About This Book

Why is this topic important?

Most experts agree that human learning, training, and performance-improvement initiatives should begin with a needs assessment that examines the relevant people-related problems and performance improvement opportunities. Human resource development and performance improvement practitioners rely on a needs assessment to develop and implement practical solutions for individuals, work groups, organizations, communities, and nations.

What can you achieve with this book?

This how-to handbook is perfect for anyone who seeks a systematic approach to assessing needs, including those who are responsible for introducing a training or development program; assessing the development needs of a workforce; improving individual, group, organization, or interorganization performance in the workplace; or providing community, national, and international development interventions.

You will read about real-life cases and tips, and about needs assessment thought leaders and their ideas and models. You will also get a treasury of tools including worksheets, ready-to-use forms, and templates for planning a course of action. The accompanying CD-ROM, which is packed with job aids, will allow you to customize the tools for your own use.

How is this book organized?

Part One begins with a bird's-eye view of needs assessment. Use the information on what needs assessment is, on the well-known models and theories of needs assessment, and on the how-tos of data collection and analysis to frame your needs assessment and to enhance your credibility with stakeholders and clients.

Part Two describes four approaches to needs assessment that can contribute greatly to success. A chapter describes each approach, including when to use the approach, and its benefits, drawbacks, and critical success factors. Where appropriate, time-saving tips are offered. Key steps are explained, and corresponding forms and worksheets in the Toolkit section are referenced.

Part Three describes strategies for managing a needs assessment. It includes ideas for writing proposals and reporting, strategies for dealing with the ethical issues that can arise when implementing a needs assessment, and answers to frequently asked questions.

Part Four contains the Needs Assessment Toolkit. It includes various templates that can be replicated and used as they are or customized by making changes on the CD-ROM included with this book.

About Pfeiffer

Pfeiffer serves the professional development and hands-on resource needs of training and human resource practitioners and gives them products to do their jobs better. We deliver proven ideas and solutions from experts in HR development and HR management, and we offer effective and customizable tools to improve workplace performance. From novice to seasoned professional, Pfeiffer is the source you can trust to make yourself and your organization more successful.

Essential Knowledge Pfeiffer produces insightful, practical, and comprehensive materials on topics that matter the most to training and HR professionals. Our Essential Knowledge resources translate the expertise of seasoned professionals into practical, how-to guidance on critical workplace issues and problems. These resources are supported by case studies, worksheets, and job aids and are frequently supplemented with CD-ROMs, websites, and other means of making the content easier to read, understand, and use.

Essential Tools Pfeiffer's Essential Tools resources save time and expense by offering proven, ready-to-use materials—including exercises, activities, games, instruments, and assessments—for use during a training or team-learning event. These resources are frequently offered in looseleaf or CD-ROM format to facilitate copying and customization of the material.

Pfeiffer also recognizes the remarkable power of new technologies in expanding the reach and effectiveness of training. While e-hype has often created whizbang solutions in search of a problem, we are dedicated to bringing convenience and enhancements to proven training solutions. All our e-tools comply with rigorous functionality standards. The most appropriate technology wrapped around essential content yields the perfect solution for today's on-the-go trainers and human resource professionals.

www.pfeiffer.com

Essential resources for training and HR professionals

THE *ASTD* MISSION:

Through exceptional learning and performance, we create a world that works better.

The American Society for Training & Development provides world-class professional development opportunities, content, networking, and resources for workplace learning and performance professionals.

Dedicated to helping members increase their relevance, enhance their skills, and align learning to business results, ASTD sets the standard for best practices within the profession.

The society is recognized for shaping global discussions on workforce development and providing the tools to demonstrate the impact of learning on the organizational bottom line. ASTD represents the profession's interests to corporate executives, policy makers, academic leaders, small business owners, and consultants through world-class content, convening opportunities, professional development, and awards and recognition.

Resources
- *T+D (Training + Development)* Magazine
- ASTD Press
- Industry Newsletters
- Research and Benchmarking
- Representation to Policy Makers

Networking
- Local Chapters
- Online Communities
- ASTD Connect
- Benchmarking Forum
- Learning Executives Network

Professional Development
- Certificate Programs
- Conferences and Workshops
- Online Learning
- CPLP™ Certification Through the ASTD Certification Institute
- Career Center and Job Bank

Awards and Best Practices
- ASTD BEST Awards
- Excellence in Practice Awards
- E-Learning Courseware Certification (ECC) Through the ASTD Certification Institute

Learn more about ASTD at www.astd.org.
1.800.628.2783 (U.S.) or 1.703.683.8100
customercare@astd.org

080615.31410

A Practical Guide *to* Needs Assessment

Second Edition

Kavita Gupta

updated and expanded by

Catherine M. Sleezer

and Darlene F. Russ-Eft

Library of Congress Cataloging-in-Publication Data

Gupta, Kavita, date.
  A practical guide to needs assessment / Kavita Gupta; updated and expanded by Catherine M. Sleezer and Darlene F. Russ-Eft.—2nd ed.
     p. cm.
  Includes bibliographical references and index.
  ISBN-13: 978-0-7879-8272-0 (cloth)
  ISBN-10: 0-7879-8272-5 (cloth)
  1. Training needs—Evaluation.   2. Needs assessment.   I. Sleezer, Catherine.   II. Russ-Eft, Darlene F.   III. Title.
  HF5549.5.T7G87 2007
  658.3'124—dc22
                                                                                              2006030501

Acquiring Editor: Matthew Davis   Director of Development: Kathleen Dolan Davies
Production Editor: Nina Kreiden   Editor: Alice Rowan
Manufacturing Supervisor: Becky Carreño   Editorial Assistant: Julie Rodriguez
Illustrations: Lotus Art

Printed in the United States of America
Printing   10   9   8   7   6   5   4   3   2
SECOND EDITION

Contents

PART FOUR: NEEDS ASSESSMENT TOOLKIT

List of Figures

List of Toolkit Forms on CD-ROM

Acknowledgments

THE PROCESS OF WRITING this book was similar to the process we describe for needs assessment; it was collaborative. Similar to any large collaborative project, the final product reflects the contributions of many people. Below we name a few.

Insights gained from reading and talking with such practitioners and researchers as James Altschuld, David Bjorkquest, Susan Fisher, Marguerite Foxon, Dana Gaines, Thomas Gilbert, Roger Kaufman, Michael Leimbach, Bob Mager, Hallie Preskill, James C. Robertson, Allison Rossett, Geary Rummler, Richard Swanson, Ryan Watkins, and Robin Yap informed our work. Co-learning with such clients, students, and colleagues as Gary Conti, Maria Cseh, Andrea Ellinger, Mary Anne Gularte, Kathleen Kelsey, Dale Kunneman, Flores Nichols, Bob Nolan, Donna Paparazzo, Melanie Spector, and Thomas Wood also informed our work.

Thanks to David Minger, Julie Suchanek, Beverly Winsch, and others who contributed cases for the book. A special thanks to the reviewers, Gary McLean, Deane Gradous, Gwyneth Tracey, Sanya Sattar, and Jeffrey White who examined the first draft with eagle eyes and provided insightful comments and suggestions.

Thanks to the staff at Pfeiffer, including Matthew C. Davis, Kathleen Dolen Davies, Nina Kreiden, Alice Rowan, Diane Turso, Ralph Lao, and Ronnie Moore, who provided competent and professional assistance every step of the way. Thanks also to Oregon State University, Oklahoma State University, and Baker Hughes–Centrilift for their support. A special thanks to our family members, who continue to provide patience, understanding, and encouragement.

Collaboration contributed to the fun of writing this edition. We hope that you find the results worthwhile.

Kavita Gupta

Catherine M. Sleezer
Baker Hughes–Centrilift

Darlene F. Russ-Eft
Oregon State University, Corvallis

Introduction

NEEDS ASSESSMENT is an important step in the performance improvement business. It precedes the design and development of any human resource development (HRD) or human performance technology (HPT) initiative. Needs assessment is a process for examining and framing people-related problems and performance improvement opportunities. It might be initiated in response to a problem or opportunity, or it might be used in ongoing learning or performance improvement efforts.

Needs assessment can focus on one or more individuals, on people within units or teams, on people across job functions, or even on an entire organization. It can also focus on the people-related problems and improvement opportunities that are an ordinary part of interorganizational, community, national, and international education, development, and performance improvement efforts.

Needs assessment relies on "insider" information about a situation. Whether we work as internal or external consultants on needs assessment with partners who have insider information about a situation, we do so to diagnose the needs accurately and to provide practical solutions to address the needs. In some cases, however, we lack the knowledge, skills, or tools to conduct an effective assessment or we are confused about which approach to use, given the wide array of choices.

PURPOSE OF THE BOOK

This book bridges the gap between needs assessment theory and practice. Over the years, scores of practitioners have expressed their frustration at the lack of resources that describe needs assessment in practitioner terms. This book, which was initially released in 1999, was a response to this frustration, and it provided a resource for the professionals who were responsible for assessing workplace needs for training, learning, organization development, and performance improvement. The book was also used by practitioners in human performance technology, human resource management, management, professional development, education, community development, and adult education.

Today, professionals who are responsible for improving learning and performance in the workplace still need practical information on how to conduct a needs assessment. However, the landscape for needs assessment has changed greatly since 1999. For example

- Organizational decisions, which are often made with great speed and communicated with a few key strokes, can have local and global impact.

- Technology plays a larger role in managing data within organizations and also provides new ways to collaborate.

- New ways to collect and share information include online surveys, e-mails, blogging, and searches of Internet documents.

- The availability of relevant ethical guidelines by professional associations has increased.

Consequently, it is time to update the book.

Today, strategic alignment within organizations is critical and data-based decision making and efficiency are more important than ever. For many organizations, strategic alignments with members of a larger community or with business partners in interorganizational efforts are just as vital.

Today's human performance problems and opportunities are complex. Seldom does one person or group have sufficient information or political support to identify and implement optimal solutions. Collaboration is required for such needs assessment efforts.

Our understanding of human performance in complex systems has also grown. Today, we better understand how organizational systems operate. We can more accurately identify the components and links that contribute to learning and performance improvement.

You will find new material throughout this second edition, but the focus remains: describing needs assessment in practitioner terms. The book still bridges the gap between needs assessment theory and practice. It still provides practitioners with how-to answers to fundamental questions such as, *How is a needs assessment done?* and *What are the steps involved in a competency-based needs assessment?* At the same time, it provides grounding from research and theory.

The first edition of the book was written by Kavita Gupta. She gave her blessing to Catherine Sleezer and Darlene Russ-Eft to update and expand on the material in the first edition, but she was not involved in writing the second edition, because she is no longer working in the area. What is new in this edition? You will find the following improvements:

- Updated needs assessment forms
- More information on the reasons for implementing a needs assessment
- More information on needs assessment models and thinking that may be especially useful when conducting a complex needs assessment
- Additional examples of needs assessments in various settings, including for-profit, nonprofit, and public sector settings; educational institutions; and organizations that offer community programs for adults

- New chapters on ethical issues, managing a needs assessment, and answers to frequently asked questions

Expert tips and case studies appear throughout the book marked with the following icons:

This icon marks an expert tip that can save you time, money, and frustration.

This icon marks a short case that demonstrates an aspect of needs assessment.

AUDIENCE FOR THE BOOK

This book is intended primarily for practitioners who are looking for systematic approaches to conducting needs assessments as the basis for the following types of initiatives:

- Introducing a training, development, or change program or initiative
- Assessing the development needs of a workforce
- Improving individual, group, organization, or interorganization performance in the workplace
- Providing community, national, and international development interventions

The book's straightforward approach is designed to keep you on target with your initiative. Its no-frills style allows you to reach the heart of the subject matter quickly and apply the principles right away.

The book is also for educators and students who want to learn more about practical approaches to needs assessment. A supplemental instructor's guide with exercises and discussion questions is available for this edition. Finally, the book is appropriate for small-business owners, family-owned businesses, and heads of small- or medium-sized organizations, including those who perform needs assessment only on an occasional basis.

SCOPE OF THE BOOK

The book lays the foundation for sound needs assessment practice through initial grounding in the whats and whys of the process. This foundation is followed by the how-tos of needs assessment. The book includes the following elements:

- A framework for understanding needs assessment and the philosophy for doing one

- Needs assessment models

- Information on how to collect and analyze data

- Step-by-step strategies for launching and implementing four needs assessment approaches

- Information on managing needs assessments

- Resources for accessing additional information

- A Toolkit containing forms and worksheets for immediate use, both in hard copy and on a CD-ROM

- A glossary to facilitate the use of a common language among HRD practitioners

HOW THE BOOK IS ORGANIZED

The book has four sections, as shown in Figure I.1.

Part One (Chapters One through Three) begins with a bird's-eye view of needs assessment. Use the information on what needs assessment is, on the well-known models and theories of needs assessment, and on the how-tos of data collection and analysis to frame your needs assessment and to enhance your credibility with stakeholders and clients.

Chapter One defines *needs assessment* and describes its key features. It also describes some challenges to assessing needs within complex systems, and it contains a matrix that compares the four needs assessment approaches that are described in the book.

Chapter Two describes practical needs assessment models and theories. It also identifies some thought leaders in the field. Being able to

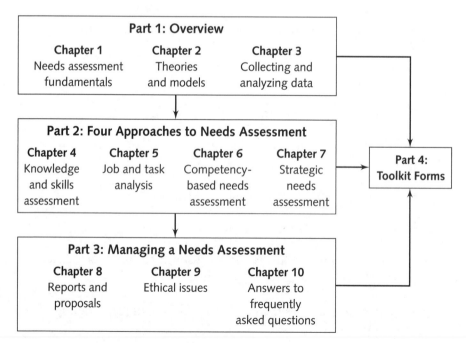

FIGURE I.1 *Overview of Book Contents*

reference these works and thought leaders can increase your credibility with clients and other stakeholders.

Chapter Three describes strategies for gathering and analyzing data. It offers guidelines for conducting interviews, focus groups, and observations. It also presents things to consider when reviewing written records and developing surveys. In addition, the chapter discusses how to analyze your needs assessment data.

Part Two (Chapters Four through Seven) describes four approaches to needs assessment that can contribute greatly to success. Each approach is described in a separate chapter that includes when to use the approach, its benefits, its drawbacks, and its critical success factors. Where appropriate, time-saving tips are offered. Key steps are explained and corresponding forms and worksheets in the Toolkit section are referenced.

Chapter Four is the first in the series of how-to chapters. It details steps for doing a conventional needs assessment to identify the knowledge and skill needs for training.

Chapter Five explains the steps for performing a job and task analysis and for formulating a training plan based on the resulting information. It also shows how to write effective job and task statements.

Chapter Six explains how to do a competency-based assessment. The steps for developing competencies using behavioral interviews are presented, and a competency dictionary and competency model are described.

Chapter Seven shows how to link performance problems and performance needs to the business strategy of an organization. Porter's (1980) five-forces model for analyzing the external environment is explained, and guidelines for using process maps are provided.

Part Three (Chapters Eight through Ten) describes strategies for managing a needs assessment. It includes ideas for writing proposals and reporting, strategies for dealing with the ethical issues that can arise when implementing a needs assessment, and answers to frequently asked questions.

Chapter Eight explains how to write proposals and reports. It also describes how to use these documents to keep a needs assessment on track.

Chapter Nine describes ethical issues that may arise when conducting a needs assessment. It also provides insights for addressing such issues.

Chapter Ten presents answers to frequently asked questions; for example, what to do about the client who does not pay or how to handle project creep. It presents practical strategies for addressing these issues.

Part Four contains the Needs Assessment Toolkit. It includes various templates that can be replicated and either used as they are or customized by making changes on the CD-ROM files included with the book.

HOW TO USE THE BOOK

This book includes basic information for those who have little prior knowledge about needs assessment, as well as more sophisticated information for experienced needs assessment practitioners who are facing complex situations. If you fall into the first category, consider reviewing all the chapters first. You can then use the information immediately or assimilate it and use it at a later date. For instance, if you want to conduct a job and task analysis for technicians right away, then consult Chapter Five. You can also use the corresponding Toolkit templates. At a later date you may want to perform a competency study for first-line supervisors. The guidelines outlined in Chapter Six, as well as the corresponding forms and worksheets, can provide a head start on this type of assessment.

If you have prior knowledge or experience with needs assessment, skim through Part One. Then focus on those chapters in Part Two that provide more in-depth information.

If you are involved in a complex needs assessment or run into problems while conducting a needs assessment, check out the models and theories in Chapter Two and the ideas for managing a needs assessment in Chapters Eight, Nine, and Ten.

This guide is designed to provide you with resources that you can tailor to your own situation. As different assessment opportunities arise in the workplace, consider using one or a combination of the approaches described in the book to proceed with your project. For a quick reference guide to the chapters, see Figure I.2.

TOOLKIT FORMS ON CD-ROM

The CD-ROM at the back of the book was designed to be used in conjunction with this second edition of *A Practical Guide to Needs Assessment*. It contains Microsoft® Word versions of the Toolkit forms found in Part Four of the book. These forms may be customized to meet your needs and used for multiple projects.

To	Consult
Review the book's contents.	Introduction
Learn what a needs assessment is, some challenges to assessing needs within complex systems, and the differences among the four approaches to needs assessment that are described in this book.	Chapter 1
Learn about practical needs assessment models and thought leaders in the field.	Chapter 2
Determine which data-gathering methods to use in a needs assessment and how to analyze the data.	Chapter 3
Link performance problems or performance needs to the business strategy of an organization.	Chapter 7
Identify training needs.	Chapters 1, 2, 4
Identify knowledge, skills, and abilities needed for a specific job or task. Develop a job description. Develop a job training plan.	Chapters 1, 2, 3, 5
Identify competencies for effective performance. Build success profiles for people, particularly in supervisory or managerial jobs. Assess gaps in proficiency levels and formulate training or performance management systems.	Chapters 1, 2, 3, 6
Develop a long-term performance improvement plan.	Chapters 1, 2, 3, 7
Write a needs assessment proposal or create in-process and final reports.	Chapter 8
Troubleshoot your needs assessment.	Chapters 2, 3, 8, 9 10

FIGURE I.2 *Quick Reference Guide to Chapters*

I

Fundamentals of Needs Assessment

ONE Overview of Needs Assessment

PURPOSE

This chapter will enable you to accomplish the following:

- Describe what a needs assessment is.
- Identify the purposes and characteristics of a needs assessment.
- Define key terms.
- Describe four approaches to needs assessment.

OVERVIEW

Most experts agree that human learning, training, and performance-improvement initiatives should begin with a needs assessment. This chapter sorts through the confusing collection of ideas about what a needs assessment really is and the best ways to conduct one. As you read the following examples of typical requests that should lead to needs assessments, think about their similarities and differences:

- *"The vice president is ready to start his personal development program. How should he proceed?"*

- *"Team production is down! The engineers say the technician team is struggling with the new process. The team disagrees. Can you give them all training or something?"*

- *"We need to update our professional certification program. What should the new curriculum include?"*

- *"Which workforce development initiatives should we invest in to make our country more competitive in the global marketplace?"*

- *"Next year our plant will continue the projects in Six Sigma quality and culture change. We will also implement new manufacturing procedures, install new equipment, and introduce new product lines. If employees try to make all these changes at once, productivity will fall. Where do you recommend we start? How can these efforts be integrated?"*

These requests probably sound familiar to most human resource development (HRD) and human performance technology (HPT) professionals. Let's consider their similarities first and then their differences. Along the way, we will discuss the characteristics of needs assessment and define some key terms.

SIMILARITIES AMONG NEEDS ASSESSMENT REQUESTS

First, did you identify *dissatisfaction with the current situation* and *desire for change* as similarities among the requests? Each request implies that a gap or discrepancy exists between what is and what could be or should be. A learning or performance gap between the current condition and the desired condition is called a need (see Figure 1.1).

Needs assessment is a process for figuring out how to close a learning or performance gap. It involves determining what the important needs are and how to address them. The process includes comparing the current condition to the desired condition, defining the problem or

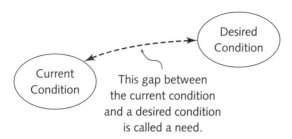

FIGURE 1.1 *Definition of a Need*

problems, understanding the behaviors and mechanisms that contribute to the current condition, determining if and how specific behaviors and mechanisms can be changed to produce the desired condition, developing solution strategies, and building support for action.

Second, did you notice the similar aims for the requests? They all focus on *addressing current issues* or on *specifying future learning or performance needs.* Needs assessment requests are typically aimed at the following situations:

- Solving a current problem

- Avoiding a past or current problem

- Creating or taking advantage of a future opportunity

- Providing learning, development, or growth

Third, did you notice that all the requests *imply a solution that requires training, learning, performance improvement, or a combination of these?* Needs assessment is a diagnostic process that relies on data collection, collaboration, and negotiation to identify and understand gaps in learning and performance and to determine future actions. Examples of actions that could be implemented as the result of a needs assessment include offering improved incentives, providing better information, engaging the appropriate people, enhancing the work design, supplying essential tools or technology, and implementing training or learning programs.

Fourth, did you also recognize that the requests are alike in including *little evidence* and *few clues* about whether taking the requested action will likely improve learning or performance? Important details about the situation and the expected course of action are unknown to both the persons who request a needs assessment and the persons who receive such requests.

Similar to the sample requests at the beginning of this section, most requests that lead to needs assessments include fuzzy goals, incompatible beliefs, flawed assumptions, and large leaps in logic. In addition, they contain *little diagnostic information* about the specific behaviors or mechanisms that produced the current condition, about what particular changes could create the desired condition, or about what support may be required from other people. Assessing needs in such situations before jumping in with solutions greatly increases the likelihood of success and avoids costly mistakes.

> **Tip**
>
> Throwing resources at problems or opportunities is like throwing a chocolate pie at the wall and hoping some of it will stick: the action is more likely to create a mess than an improvement; furthermore, it is a waste of good resources.

Finally, did you notice that all the sample requests include *challenging questions?* The right answers to these questions cannot be found in a book or on the Internet. Indeed, such questions do not have one right answer. Using commonsense solutions or throwing resources at such situations seldom work well either.

Instead, the requests for learning, training, and performance improvement initiatives must be evaluated and the "merit, worth, or value" (Scriven, 1991, p. 139) of the various options must be analyzed. Thus, needs assessment is a type of evaluation.

The Systems Model of Evaluation (Preskill & Russ-Eft, 2003; Russ-Eft & Preskill, 2005) identifies various factors that affect the success and the outcomes of an evaluation, including a needs assessment (see Figure 1.2). Factors in the needs assessment or evaluation project itself (such as the approach to managing the project) are shown in the model's inner circle; factors within the organization (such as the organization's mission, vision, and strategic goals) are shown in the model's outer circle; and factors that are outside the organization (such as customer expectations) are shown in the shapes that encircle the ring of organizational factors. Thus many factors can influence how the challenging questions raised by a needs assessment are answered.

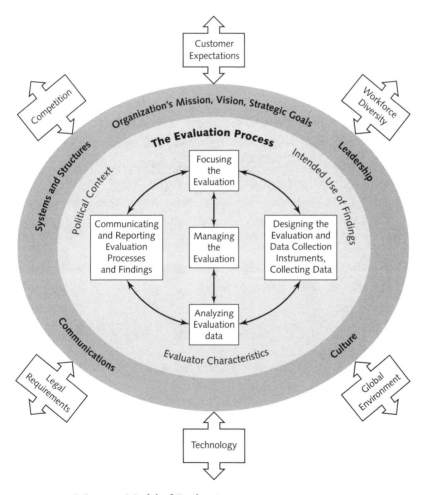

FIGURE 1.2 *A Systems Model of Evaluation*

Reprinted with permission from Sage, appearing in Russ-Eft, D., and Preskill, H. (2005). In search of the Holy Grail: ROI evaluation in HRD. *Advances in Developing Human Resources,* 71–85.

We have considered the similarities among the requests that lead needs assessment. Next, we consider their differences.

DIFFERENCES AMONG REQUESTS THAT LEAD TO NEEDS ASSESSMENT

First, did you notice that the sample requests *target different levels of learning and performance?* Needs assessment can be used to diagnose the learning and performance needs of individuals, teams, functional units, and whole organizations. They can also be used to diagnose the people-related issues of interorganizational groups, communities, countries, and even international efforts.

Second, did you notice that the requests focus on *various aspects of learning and performance?* Learning is the act of gaining knowledge or skills. It can exist in the individual and it can reside in an organization's systems, databases, technologies, and culture. Training supports individual learning (that is, a gain in knowledge and skills) through specialized instruction and practice. The terms *knowledge* and *skill* have different meanings:

- *Knowledge:* The body of facts about a subject matter and the understanding that a person acquires through study or experience

- *Skill:* Knowledge that one proficiently applies in appropriate situations

The goalie in Figure 1.3 may have in-depth knowledge of soccer rules and the various plays allowed in the game. His role on the team is to prevent the ball from going into the net and allowing the opposing team to score. The picture shows that he has failed to block several balls.

Performance includes accomplishments, the processes that result in accomplishments, and the capacity for future performance. Let us consider each of these aspects of performance for our soccer goalie:

FIGURE 1.3 *Soccer Player Who Knows Game's Rules but Lacks Game's Skills*

- *Accomplishment:* The major accomplishment desired for the goalie during the game is to save the goal by preventing the ball from going into the net.

- *Process:* To save the goal, the goalie integrates his knowledge of how to play the position with such skills as deflecting the ball and falling on it. His knowledge and skills interact with other factors (such as the defensive skills of his teammates) to affect how well he carries out the process of playing goalie.

- *Capacity:* The goalie's capacity for performance includes his bundle of skills and resources that can be applied to future play. They indicate his abilities to apply his mental, physical, and social skills to add value to the team.

The goalie's accomplishments, processes, and capacity could affect the team's accomplishments (for example, the number of games won), their processes (such as the strategies the team uses while playing the game), and their capacity (that is, the team's bundle of skills and resources that can be applied to future play).

Some people see learning and performance as separate activities. We see them as interconnected. As seen in the example of the goalie, learning in the form of knowledge and skills can affect performance and vice versa. Although, learning is not directly observable, the behaviors that create performance can often be observed. Thus, changes in behavior are often used to infer that learning has occurred. For example, if our goalie observed a new technique, practiced the technique, and in subsequent games effectively used that technique, we could infer that learning had occurred.

This section has described the similarities and differences among sample requests that lead to needs assessments, and in the process described the characteristics of needs assessments and defined some key terms. Next we focus on the benefits of needs assessment.

BENEFITS OF A NEEDS ASSESSMENT

A needs assessment frames the problems or opportunities of interest and builds relationships among the people and groups who have a stake in the issue. It also provides the foundation for planning and action to improve learning, training, and performance. More specifically, a needs assessment can align resources with strategy, build relationships among those who have a stake in the situation, clarify problems or opportunities, set goals for future action, and provide data for decision making. A needs assessment can also identify leverage points and resources for making changes, establish objectives for initiatives, prioritize actions, determine who must be involved for the HRD and HPT efforts to be successful, and provide baseline data for later evaluation of results.

Equally important, a needs assessment can build support for HRD and HPT efforts. The processes of using accurate data and negotiating among differing points of view can engage and mobilize decision makers and others who have a stake in the situation. By sharing their knowledge, insights, and resources, those who are closest to the situation contribute to creating solutions that are practical, credible, and appropriate for the situation.

Given all of these benefits, it is obvious why so many training, learning, and performance improvement models advocate systematic needs assessment: it ensures that interventions are relevant and address the needs.

FOUR APPROACHES TO NEEDS ASSESSMENT

Needs assessments are particularly important to HRD and HPT professionals who must align their work with strategic individual, organizational, or community needs. In today's competitive climate, improving learning, training, and performance is emphasized more than ever before.

At the same time, individuals, organizations, and communities guard their resources. Today's decision makers want HRD and HPT initiatives to focus on their critical priorities and to drop the non-value-added work. Needs assessments can provide such a focus, but politics will affect how needs assessments are actually conducted.

Consider the situation facing Ruth Duple, the new manager of learning and organization development for an international firm that manufactures computer equipment. The firm's management team recently speculated that poor supervisory performance was causing quality problems, increased turnover, and missed production deadlines. They handed the problem to Ruth. When she reviewed this new challenge, Ruth realized that she did not know how the poor supervisory performance related to the organization's strategic goals, the cause or causes of the problems, or the management team's vision for supervisory performance.

Tip

Some people focus on the problems in a situation, while others recognize that the same problems present opportunities for improvement.

To aid her thinking, Ruth sketched a simplified systems diagram of her firm (see Figure 1.4). The large oval represents the firm. Note that it is bordered with dashed lines to acknowledge that changes from outside the firm (such as government regulations, politics, and raw materials) can affect the firm, and that changes from inside the firm (such as increased wages) can affect the larger environment. Inputs to the firm's performance system include the employees, tools, and raw materials (such as gears).

Within the firm, each gray box represents a distinct unit or department that contributes to the production process. Of course the firm actually has many more units than are shown in Figure 1.4. Employees in each unit use work processes (shown by the darker gray horizontal boxes) to convert materials and other inputs into unit outputs. The outputs of one unit become the inputs for other units. When all the production processes are complete, the firm's output—computer equipment—is loaded on trucks for shipment to customers.

The employees in each unit report to a supervisor who in turn reports to a manager. The managers and some other executives report to the firm's CEO.

For the sake of simplicity, Ruth did not include in her sketch the collaborative efforts that span units, the feedback that supervisors receive from internal and external customers and from managers, or the firm's

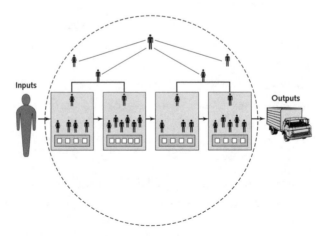

FIGURE 1.4 *Ruth's Sketch of a Simplified Systems Diagram*

structure, politics, and culture. However, her sketch does provide a focus for thinking about the needs assessment.

As an experienced HRD professional, Ruth knows many needs assessment models, each with its own jargon and unique steps. She is also familiar with the needs assessment study by Mathews et al. (2001). It focused on organizations in the United Kingdom, Finland, and Portugal that were implementing quality management practices such as ISO 9001:2000. The study ranked the importance of the following elements to assessing training needs within an organization:

- Senior management decisions
- Supervisors' opinions
- Skills inventory
- Employee surveys
- Analysis of projected business or service plans
- Customer opinions
- Training audits
- Requests from work groups
- External consultant
- Advisory committee

The study found that senior management decisions and supervisors' opinions received much higher rankings than the other elements, indicating the importance of the senior management and supervisors in determining training needs. The authors recommended that objective and formal methods of assessing needs be more widely adopted. This study highlights that while management and supervisor perspectives are important, using objective data and formal methods could ensure broader support for addressing quality management practices.

Ruth's firm must address its quality problems, increased turnover, and missed production deadlines to remain competitive in today's marketplace.

Given the competitive importance of these issues, Ruth decided to use a formal needs assessment approach to gain more knowledge about the gap between actual and desired supervisory performance and to figure out how to close it. She considered four formal needs assessment approaches that can be used separately or in combination.

The first approach, *knowledge and skills assessment,* focuses on the knowledge and skill needs that may exist. If such needs do exist, they can be addressed with training. Ruth could survey the supervisors themselves to obtain a list of their knowledge and skill needs or she could talk to managers. Ruth could then implement training programs that address the needs. This approach to needs assessment is described in Chapter Four.

The second approach, *job and task analysis,* focuses on information about the scope, responsibilities, and tasks of particular job functions. Because Ruth knows that supervisors regularly mishandle performance reviews, she could implement a job and task analysis to gather specific information about how this supervisory job task should be conducted in the firm. Ruth could use this needs assessment approach to prioritize the knowledge, skills, and other improvements that are required to close the gap between the way the performance reviews are conducted and the way they should be conducted. This approach to needs assessment is described in Chapter Five.

The third approach, *competency-based needs assessment,* focuses on determining the competencies needed for specific job functions. Competencies are the knowledge, skills, attitudes, values, motivations, and beliefs that people must have to be successful in a job. Ruth knows that successful supervisors are those whose teams continually outperform other teams and whose subordinates tend to remain with the organization. Ruth could use this needs assessment approach to identify specific behaviors that are exhibited by successful supervisors and not exhibited by less successful supervisors. This approach to needs assessment is described in Chapter Six.

The fourth approach, *strategic needs assessment,* focuses on learning and performance gaps within the context of an organization's business strategy. Ruth could use this needs assessment approach to learn how supervisors do and do not contribute to the unit's and the firm's strategic goals and about the work mechanisms that contribute to their current performance. She could also consider factors in the firm's external and internal environments. Ruth could use the information she gathers to map the desired work processes and outcomes, to develop supervisory training, and to address non-training issues. This approach to needs assessment is described in Chapter Seven.

Figure 1.5 is a graph of the time and labor required to complete each of the four approaches. The approaches in the lower portion of the chart are less time- and labor-intensive. Figure 1.6 summarizes the approaches presented in Figure 1.5, starting with the lower-most approach, describing when to use each approach and its advantages and disadvantages.

Regardless of which approach you decide to use, consider the realities of conducting needs assessments in the workplace. First, time will always be a critical factor, as most clients or sponsors will be more concerned about implementing the actual improvement than about spending time analyzing needs. Second, line managers may be reluctant to release personnel to participate in interviews or focus groups, especially if operations will be affected. Third, needs assessments are political. Individuals hold differing and sometimes conflicting opinions, and they use power and influence to achieve their own ends. Therefore, a needs assessment usually involves negotiating cooperation among people to achieve a common task.

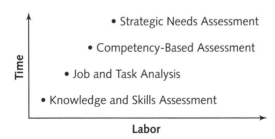

FIGURE 1.5 *Effort Required for the Needs Assessment Approaches*

Approach	Purpose	When to Use	Advantages	Disadvantages
Knowledge and Skills Assessment	Identify the knowledge and skills required to perform a job	Implement new technology Identify training needs Develop a training plan	Ensures training is linked to the learner's needs Easiest to implement	Has a limited focus
Job and Task Analysis	Determine responsibilities and tasks necessary to perform a job	Develop new job descriptions or revise existing position profiles Identify task listings for new or redesigned job functions: knowledge, skills, abilities, and standards Develop consistent training requirements, especially for technical and specialized jobs	Stimulates interest because people have opportunity to define jobs Defines skill requirements for entry-level versus senior positions Identifies additional knowledge, skills, and abilities to move across or upward within a job function	Does not take into account the external factors that may affect job performance Time-consuming Costly Assumes that the work is static Assumes that there is one best way to perform the work

Competency-Based Needs Assessment	Identify knowledge, skills, and attitudes for superior job performance	Identify competencies that are required for jobs Measure proficiency levels of people Develop standardized training Develop performance management systems (recruiting, hiring, promoting, or career planning)	Determines qualities that distinguish average from superior performance Provides information about current and future predictors of job performance	Time-consuming Requires high involvement of many people within an organization Costly Requires good project management system for large projects
Strategic Needs Assessment	Examine existing performance problems (reactive) or address new and future performance needs (proactive) within the context of the organization's or the community's business strategy Develop long-term performance improvement plan	Link performance improvement needs to business strategy of the organization or community Identify performance improvement opportunities at various levels (such as individual, process, and organizational)	Develops long-term solutions to existing performance problems or new performance needs Solves problems that affect core business processes Eliminates non-value-added activities	Time-consuming Costly Requires that a business strategy exist

FIGURE 1.6 *Matrix of Needs Assessment Approaches*

After considering the four approaches, Ruth concluded that this could be a high-stakes needs assessment both for the firm and for her career. Because of the project's importance, Ruth decided to review the needs assessment tools presented in the next chapter before selecting a needs assessment approach.

CONCLUSION

Needs assessment involves carefully analyzing a situation and building support for action. Regardless of which needs assessment approach you choose to implement, the message is simple: needs assessments set the direction for learning, training, and performance improvement initiatives. The next chapter describes some practical models and thinking that can contribute greatly to a successful needs assessment.

TWO | Ideas and Models That Guide Practice

PURPOSE

This chapter will enable you to accomplish the following:

- Recognize the difference between needs and wants.
- Identify different kinds of needs.
- Recognize different kinds of assessments.
- Recognize the pioneers in the needs assessment field.
- Add clout to your needs assessments with powerful ideas and models.

OVERVIEW

Why should you take the time to learn about needs assessment ideas and models? Because they can make your job easier and add great value to your needs assessment! Today's learning and performance improvement situations are complex. Moreover, HRD and HPT initiatives are key drivers of growth, transformation, and productivity for individuals, organizations, communities, and countries. In this high-stakes environment, knowing need assessment ideas and models that provide the language and insights for success is simply smart practice.

You should also know the names of the pioneers who contributed significantly to our current understanding of needs assessment; for example, Thomas Gilbert, Joe Harless, Roger Kaufman, Robert Mager, Allison Rossett, Geary Rummler, and Richard Swanson. As you read this chapter and other chapters in this book, watch for their names.

The ideas and models presented in this chapter can be used in conjunction with the approaches to needs assessment described in Chapters Four, Five, Six, and Seven. The ideas and models are grouped into three categories based on use: (1) prioritizing needs, (2) measuring performance, and (3) finding the causes of problems.

> **Tip**
>
> During initial meetings with the client or decision makers to contract a needs assessment, be prepared, if asked, to discuss needs assessment ideas, models, and pioneers. Most decision makers carefully select the analyst who conducts their assessment, and they often rely on informal discussions of these topics to select practitioners who have the appropriate and in-depth knowledge.

PRIORITIZING NEEDS

Most individuals, teams, organizations, communities, and countries have more *wants* and *needs* than available resources to address them. Use the information in this section to quickly separate needs from wants, distinguish among various kinds of need, and consider the analysis the project requires.

A want is something the client would like to have even though it does not contribute to the long-term learning or performance goal. By contrast, a need, when addressed, contributes to achieving the desired learning or performance goal by closing the gaps between the current condition and the desired condition. Thus, important questions for any proposed needs assessment are, *Whose needs will the project address?* and *What kind of needs will the project address?*

Because needs assessments are implemented in complex systems, a change in one level or element of the system can affect other levels and elements. For example, a needs assessment within an organization can produce results that contribute to the larger shared society (Kaufman, 2005). However, practitioners should carefully consider the focus for a needs assessment before starting any project. Three kinds of needs that you are likely to see in practice and that warrant a needs assessment are as follows:

- *Strategic or operational business needs.* These are gaps between current and desired conditions relative to achieving a business strategy. Closing these gaps is critical for the long-term success of the entity or its units.

- *Individual performance needs.* These are gaps between current and desired conditions relative to a person's accomplishments, behaviors, or capacity for performance. An individual sometimes closes such gaps to meet personal goals or to meet strategic or operational business goals.

- *Learning needs.* These are gaps in knowledge and skill between the current and desired conditions. Most needs assessment experts agree that individuals have learning needs. In addition, growing bodies of literature describe team and organizational learning needs.

Other kinds of needs may involve various groups (such as specific teams or departments, organizational units, or community and national groups) and different foci (such as sales performance or community collaboration and development).

When determining which needs to address first, keep in mind that interventions will be perceived as valuable only if they contribute to reducing the need by providing a solution. Usually the strategic or operational business needs are assessed for an entity before other kinds of needs are assessed. The ultimate goal of interventions in private sector organizations is usually increased profitability (reduced costs and time, improved quality, or increased revenues), and the goal of interventions in public sector organizations is usually fuller achievement of the mission or the funding goals.

The kind of need and the context influence the type of analysis that should be conducted:

- *Business analysis:* To identify an organization's strategic or operational goals, clarify that they are appropriate and determine how to measure them.

- *Performance analysis:* To identify the capacity and processes for producing accomplishments, to ensure that performance requirements and changes are linked to organizational strategic or operational goals, and to ensure that performers have the support they need to achieve the goals.

- *Cause analysis:* To identify the specific reasons for performance gaps.

- *Training needs assessment:* To identify the performance gaps that can be addressed with training solutions. This type of analysis is usually conducted for providers of training solutions. It identifies the training gaps and the non-training gaps that influence the effectiveness with which the performance gaps can be closed.

MEASURING PERFORMANCE

Some people claim that it is impossible to measure performance precisely or to establish its values. They are correct. Other people claim that not all HRD and HPT initiatives are designed to produce economic value. They are also correct.

We find, however, that most people rely on less-than-perfect measures to make decisions and that they do indeed place economic values on learning and performance when making such decisions as selecting products to use, choosing strategies for accomplishing tasks, assigning people to participate in projects, and selecting needs to address. One key to making better decisions is to share the expectations, criteria, and formulas for measuring and valuing performance.

Gilbert's (1978) Behavior Engineering Model (BEM) is the classic model for measuring performance. It describes the relationships among behaviors, accomplishments, and performance. Behaviors are what people do, accomplishments are their outputs, and individual performance includes both behaviors and accomplishments. Consider the following three examples:

- In a restaurant, three waiters serve meals.
- In a garage, ten mechanics repair autos.
- In a clinic, twenty physicians treat patients.

The accomplishments in these examples are the served meals, repaired autos, and treated patients. The behaviors are the specific actions taken by the individuals who served meals, repaired autos, and treated patients. According to the BEM, an individual's performance reflects both valued accomplishments and the costs of their behaviors.

Tip

When measuring performance, first look at the desired condition and then identify and measure the accomplishments that contribute to reaching it. Then analyze the behaviors that contribute to the accomplishment.

To measure performance efficiently among the individuals in a group, try this Gilbert (1978) strategy:

1. Compare the accomplishments of typical and outstanding performers.

2. Identify patterns in their accomplishments. (For example, have the typical and outstanding performers reached the same levels of accomplishment? What are the differences in their patterns?)

3. Find the specific behaviors that contribute to the patterns.

When typical and outstanding performers work in the same environment, their differences in accomplishment are often the result of small differences in their behaviors. The following case shows a real-life example of such differences.

Case

A needs assessment at a call center for a provider of telephone services relied on comparing typical and outstanding performance. The call center's mission was to increase the satisfaction and retention of the customers who had complaints. A strategic goal was to address 99 percent of all customer complaints effectively and efficiently. However, the employees who recorded customer complaints often misrecorded their addresses and phone numbers, making it difficult to follow up with customers.

Measuring and comparing the accomplishments of employees who worked the call lines revealed that one outstanding employee had a far higher level of accomplishment than the other employees as measured by the number of customer complaints accurately and quickly entered into the call center's database.

Further investigation revealed that the outstanding employee used different behaviors than the typical employees. For example, when a customer called in a complaint, the outstanding employee asked about their contact information and typed changes into the call center database at about seventy words per minute. She also repeated the contact information back to customers while entering it into the database, thus ensuring accuracy. By comparison, typical employees usually had to hunt and peck to locate the correct keys for entering data, and they did not repeat back to the customer the changes they had entered into the database.

The call center supervisor knew that the average number of missed service calls due to this issue was fifteen per week and the average costs for technicians who drove around but could not find the customer was $110 (wages and transportation). To calculate the annual cost of poor performance, the supervisor multiplied fifteen by $110 times fifty weeks per year to get $85,800. These costs were so high that the supervisor did not even bother calculating the average worth of dissatisfied customers who chose a new telephone company when technicians did not solve their problems.

Instead, he improved unit performance by using a two-pronged intervention that (a) provided training on keyboarding skills to employees who needed them and (b) changed the work design so that everyone who answered customer complaints repeated changes in contact information while entering them into the computer. The total cost for these changes was around $5,000.

Today, performance improvements are typically measured using *return-on-investment* (ROI). This formula compares the investment in a program with its return.

ROI = program benefits minus costs/program costs × 100

For example, to calculate the ROI for a program with a $85,800 benefit and a $5,000 cost, first calculate that $85,800 minus $5,000 equals $80,800. Then divide $80,800 by $5,000 and multiply the result by 100. This equals 16.16 percent. For each $1 invested, the return is $16.

> **Tip**
>
> When measuring accomplishments, such soft measures as improved teamwork or innovation can be converted into hard numbers by considering exactly how the accomplishment affects mission-critical work. Resources that offer specific strategies for completing such conversions include *Forecasting the Financial Benefits of HRD,* by Swanson and Gradous (1990), and *Measuring Return on Investment (ROI) Basics,* by Phillips and Phillips (2005).

DIAGNOSING THE CAUSES OF POOR PERFORMANCE

Learning and performance needs may be only vaguely understood when they first come to our attention. Moreover, as Harless (1970) often observed, organizations—when confronted with problems—tend to look for solutions even before the problem is fully defined or alternate courses of action have been considered. Harless recommended front-end analysis for uncovering the root causes of performance problems prior to looking for solutions. We now examine the root causes of individual, organizational, and systems problems.

Individual Performance Problems

When individuals do not perform as expected, organizations often train them or remove them. Mager and Pipe (1984) differentiated between performance problems that result from a skill deficiency and those that result from other causes (such as lack of motivation or obstacles to performing). There is little point to providing individuals with knowledge and skills if the lack of performance is caused by low motivation or obstacles to performing (such as lack of resources).

Gilbert (1978) identified six barriers to performance for individuals. Figure 2.1 shows the six variables and sample questions for identifying whether a variable is a barrier. The traditional assumption is that if an individual performer would simply change, improvement would result (for example, "if he were not so lazy," or "if she could do the work," or "if they just had the knowledge and skills. . . ."). However, performance problems more often result from a lack of support in the work environment (for example, bad data, worn-out tools, or poor incentives).

For instance, the expensive software purchased by a school system to improve student reading skills received little use even though the teachers in the system had received training on how to use the software. The expected performance did not appear until the school superintendent dialogued with teachers about how using the software could improve student learning, supplied sufficient computers, and provided feedback on the level of the software use in each classroom.

Barriers to Performance	Sample Question About the Barrier
1. Data	Does the individual have sufficient and reliable information (such as purpose and expectations for the job and feedback on performance) to guide performance?
2. Tools	Does the individual have all the resources needed to perform the work?
3. Incentives	Are the financial and nonfinancial incentives adequate and based on performance?
4. Knowledge	Is lack of knowledge (or skill) contributing to the problem?
5. Capacity	Do the individual's physical, emotional, and intellectual abilities match the job requirements?
6. Motives	Does the person have the appropriate motives to perform this work well?

FIGURE 2.1 *Barriers to Performance and Sample Questions*

Organizational Performance Problems

Diagnosing an organization's problems is complex. Here we review two models that can aid you in this process.

The Organization Elements Model

In the *Organization Elements Model (OEM),* needs assessment and strategic planning are used to link and define an organization's desired external and internal results (Kaufman, 1992, 2005). Elements in the OEM include the following:

- *Inputs:* The resources an organization uses
- *Processes:* The internal ways, means, methods, activities, and procedures an organization uses to achieve desired results
- *Products:* The results produced within an organization
- *Outputs:* The end results delivered outside an organization
- *Outcomes:* The effects or payoffs for clients and society

You can use the OEM diagram in Figure 2.2 to compare the current situation and the desired situation across all five elements, thus obtaining information about the organization (the inputs, process, and products), the external clients (the outputs), and the societal context (the outcomes).

Improving Performance: Managing the White Space on the Organizational Chart

With the publication of their book *Improving Performance* in 1995, Rummler and Brache revolutionized the practice of needs assessment in organizations. Instead of referring to a traditional organizational chart with its departmental silos, they described an organization as a system with such components as inputs, a processing system, outputs, markets, and shareholders.

	Inputs	Process	Products	Outputs	Outcomes
What should be					
What is					

FIGURE 2.2 *Organization Elements Model Diagram*

Source: Kaufman, 1992.

They also showed how to depict the interrelationships between departments. Figure 2.3 compares a traditional view and a systems view of an organization. Needs assessment practitioners who understand the systems view of organizations can move beyond focusing on activities that occur within departmental silos to focusing on activities that occur across departments.

Rummler and Brache also described the importance of diagnosing performance needs that occur at three levels: the organization, the processes, and the individual jobs and performers. Because the three levels are interdependent and critical to the whole system's optimal performance, a failure of any one can affect the ability of the organization to perform optimally. Today most needs assessment practitioners recognize that organizations are systems comprised of subsystems. Moreover, many practitioners and decision makers refer to the three levels of performance that were first identified by Rummler and Brache.

> **Tip**
>
> Most people who use systems thinking in their work acknowledge that *no* single systemic tool depicts the whole truth about a situation.

Diagnosing Systems

Our knowledge about how to analyze complex systems has improved greatly in recent years. Eoyang (2004) presented strategies and tools for assessing the patterns that occur within systems:

1. *Surface structures* are patterns visible to anyone in the organization and easily measured (for example, lagging sales, interpersonal conflict, and client dissatisfaction).

2. *Evident deep structures* are patterns that are partially or totally invisible but easily measured (for example, the beliefs shared by members of the organization about its mission).

3. *Subtle deep structures* are patterns that are invisible and not easily measured (for example, data points that occur at different places and are distributed across time).

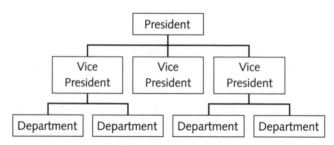

Traditional View of an Organization

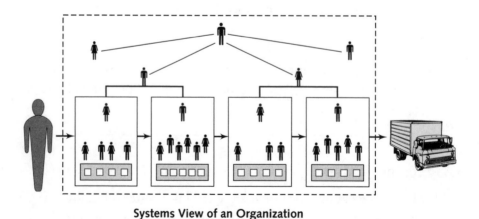

Systems View of an Organization

FIGURE 2.3 *Comparison of the Traditional and Systems Views of an Organization*

Toolkit Form 2.1 shows assessment tools and strategies for each of the three categories. You can use it to become more intentional in imagining multiple options for each type of system pattern.

CONCLUSION

The ideas and models described in this chapter can be used with the four approaches presented in this book. Select the ones that best fit your situation and use them to cut through the complexities in your situation. The next chapter describes strategies for collecting and analyzing data.

THREE

Strategies for Collecting and Analyzing Data

PURPOSE

This chapter will enable you to do the following:

- Prepare for and conduct individual interviews.
- Conduct focus groups.
- Make observations.
- Develop and use surveys.
- Gather data from documents and artifacts.
- Compare features of interviews, focus groups, surveys, and observations.
- Identify strategies for analyzing data.
- Identify ways to communicate findings.

OVERVIEW

Needs assessment results reflect the methods that were used to collect the data and the methods that were used to analyze it. Thus, data collection and analysis are cornerstone skills of any needs assessment project.

Most needs assessments rely on multiple data-collection methods. To identify the training needs of plant personnel, you could choose to conduct interviews. To measure the proficiency levels of field engineers, you could choose to conduct a survey *and* observe them at work. This chapter will help you decide which methods are most appropriate and will provide guidelines for using the methods. It also describes how to analyze the data after they have been collected to produce accurate and useable results. While you can hire experts who specialize in data collection and analysis methods (such as statistics and survey design), most methods are straightforward to learn.

Needs assessment is the first phase of the professional development model used by the Jefferson County Public Schools in Louisville, Kentucky. The needs assessment determines what professional development is needed, why it is needed, who needs it, and what knowledge, skills, and improved performance will result. Sources of data for the needs assessment include observations, interviews, surveys, and reviews of written documents.

DATA-COLLECTION METHODS

The data-collection methods discussed in this chapter are interviews, focus groups, surveys, observations, and archival records. Additional methods, such as the nominal group technique, action research, and Dacum (developing a curriculum) are beyond the scope of this chapter. For real-life applications of these latter data-gathering techniques, consult *In Action: Conducting Needs Assessment* (Phillips & Holton, 1995).

Interviews

Some people assume that interviews are one of the easiest tools for gathering information about learning and performance needs. A brief discussion with customer service associates could uncover reasons why phone calls are not being handled properly. An in-depth discussion with senior management could clarify perspectives on strategic training issues. However, such interviews can be challenging; a certain amount of knowledge and skill is involved in conducting informative interviews.

Types of Interviews

Interviews can be conducted in person, by phone, or by computer technology (such as online cameras, videoconferencing, and instant messaging). The greatest benefit of one-on-one, in-person interviews is the human interaction that occurs. In-person interviews allow the interviewer to observe facial expressions and other nonverbal cues from respondents.

Phone interviews are useful when people in remote locations cannot be accessed easily. They are also useful when people do not have the time and resources to travel to meet in person. Because most people will refuse to participate in long phone interviews, phone interviews are typically scheduled to last no longer than thirty minutes. Such time limitations clearly reduce the amount of information that can be gathered. Therefore, phone interview is not the optimal choice when extensive discussion is likely.

Computer-aided telephone interviewing can be used for some interviews; the text appears on the computer screen for the interviewer along with the response options, and the interviewer can enter the interviewee's responses. In addition to computer-aided telephone interviewing, computer-supported interviews can be a good choice when people are comfortable using technology such as online cameras and videoconferencing. With these aids, as with in-person interviews, the interviewer can observe nonverbal cues and, as with phone interviews, people do not have to travel to meet in person.

Whether conducting interviews in person, by phone, or using computer technology, it is useful to remember the following tips:

- Use a moderate tone.

- Enunciate clearly.

- Avoid speaking rapidly.
- Keep the discussion focused.
- Probe for additional responses to your questions.

Interview Approaches

Interviews can be structured (or scripted), unstructured, or semistructured. In structured interviews, a list of objectives and a corresponding list of questions guide the interview process. In unstructured interviews, questions are not listed in advance. Rather, a list of objectives and topics to be covered guide the interview. In semistructured interviews, a list of objectives with corresponding questions initially guide the interview and the interviewer spontaneously asks supplemental questions to explore further areas of interest.

In structured or scripted interviews, the interview dialogue and the questions, and in some cases the responses to closed-ended questions, are written out and practiced in advance. Scripts are useful when multiple interviewers are involved in the data-gathering process and when using computer-aided interviewing. A script can be combined with a protocol that details all data-collection procedures (for example, how interviewees are initially contacted, interview follow-up procedures, and the confidentiality agreement). Scripted interviews help to ensure accuracy and consistency of the interview process. They may, however, inhibit spontaneity. Figure 3.1 shows a sample interview protocol, the script, and the sample questions.

Keys to a successful interview include preparing for it and developing questions before actually conducting the interview. Some people prepare for the interview before developing questions and some people develop questions first. Figures 3.2, 3.3, and 3.4 present tips for each of these tasks.

Focus Groups

In the focus group interview method, people who have something in common are brought together and asked their opinions and ideas about a specific topic. Most focus groups are made up of five to eight people.

Protocol

These interviews are conducted as part of a strategic needs assessment that focuses on customer perceptions of a manufacturing division. The performance improvement specialist will conduct interviews during the next week with all the direct reports of the vice president of manufacturing. The administrative assistant will schedule the interviews. All interview responses will be grouped for reporting to the president and the vice president of manufacturing and are therefore anonymous. The interview script and sample questions will guide the activity; as issues surface, additional questions may be asked. The collected data will be analyzed by identifying themes.

Interview Script

Thank you for agreeing to see me. The purpose of this interview is to discuss the recent customer survey and to get your views for the strategic needs assessment. I am interviewing all of the direct reports of the vice president of manufacturing. I will group the responses from all the interviews before reporting the results to the president and vice president of manufacturing, so your responses to questions will be anonymous. I have a list of questions to get us started and there may be other questions as we talk. Would you like to see the list of questions?

Sample Questions

1. What do you think about the recent customer survey?
2. What changes in our production process do you think we should make to address our weaknesses and improve our strengths?
3. What other factors outside the organization could lead to changes in our production process? Follow-up: What could the changes look like?
4. Are there other factors inside the organization that could lead to changes in our production process? Follow-up: What could the changes look like?
5. What are the barriers to making efficient and effective changes in the production process?
6. What are the supports for making efficient and effective changes in the production process?
7. In thinking about our future production process, what additional information should be considered?
8. Do you have any additional thoughts on the customer survey?
9. Thank you for meeting with me to discuss the strategic needs for the production area. If I think of additional questions later or need clarification on a question, can I call you?

FIGURE 3.1 *Sample Interview Protocol, Script, and Questions*

1. Familiarize yourself with technical and industry-specific terms.
2. Obtain background information about the problem or issue of concern if possible.
3. Establish the purpose, expected outcomes, and objectives for the interview.
4. Determine whether the interview will be conducted in person, by phone, or online.
5. Identify a comfortable and private location for conducting a one-on-one, in-person interview.
6. Decide how information will be recorded. Handwritten notes? Typing responses into computer? Tape recording? Video recording?
7. Test the equipment that will be used.
8. Develop an interview protocol if multiple interviewers will be involved.
9. Notify interviewees and their managers or supervisors of the interviews.
10. Send a letter of introduction to each interviewee that states the objectives of the interview:
    a. Explain why he or she was selected.
    b. Specify whether confidentiality will be maintained.
    c. Explain how the results will be used.
11. Specify a time when you will call to schedule an interview appointment.
12. Call the interviewee to schedule the interview.
13. Allow twenty to thirty minutes between interviews to document the results.
14. Allow flexibility in scheduling to accommodate those working in shifts.

FIGURE 3.2 *Tips for Preparing for an Interview*

1. Place easy-to-answer, open-ended questions at the beginning. This will help the interviewee to begin talking and can help to develop trust and rapport.
2. Place important questions near the beginning of the interview.
3. Place controversial or sensitive questions, including demographic questions, at the end.
4. Specify the amount of time to be spent on each question.
5. Ensure that each question matches a stated objective.
6. Sequence questions from general to specific.
7. Sequence and cluster questions in a logical order.
8. Ensure that questions are clear, concise, and jargon-free.
9. Be sure that questions are appropriate for the skill and experience levels of the target audience.
10. Provide adequate space between questions to record information.
11. Pilot-test interview questions.
12. Make appropriate revisions.

FIGURE 3.3 *Tips for Developing Interview Questions*

1. Begin with a few rapport-building questions.
2. Obtain permission to record the interview.
3. Avoid adhering rigidly to the question sequence. Be flexible, but ensure that all questions have been covered by the end. If they have not been, schedule a follow-up phone or online interview.
4. Give all participants an equal amount of time to respond to each question.
5. Clarify responses when necessary.
6. Ask for concrete examples to support statements.
7. Separate facts from opinions, if possible.
8. Maintain a neutral attitude.
9. Avoid discussing results with other interviewees.
10. Ask whether interviewees have additional questions or comments at the end.
11. Offer appreciation for participation.
12. Summarize key points.
13. Ask whether interviewees can be contacted again if necessary.

FIGURE 3.4 *Tips for Conducting an Interview*

To be effective, focus groups require skilled facilitators. Krueger and Casey (2000) noted that a facilitator must be mentally prepared, familiar with such techniques as the five-second pause and probing for more information, and able to show positive regard and empathy for participants. As Schwarz (1995) pointed out, focus group facilitators must keep in mind that they are not content experts, mediators, arbitrators, or judges. Schwarz's suggestions for facilitators included the following:

- Accept responses in a nonjudgmental manner.
- Avoid making decisions or comments about a group's work.
- Encourage an atmosphere of openness and mutual respect.

The work of conducting needs assessments via focus groups involves three phases: prepare, conduct, and report.

Prepare

Preparing for a focus group involves several activities. First, the facilitator becomes familiar with the purpose of the focus group and its expected outcomes, the topic of interest, and any specific terminology or jargon that is likely to be used. Second, the facilitator develops and pilot-tests a list of questions that will encourage focus group participants to disclose information on the topic. In a few cases, the facilitator creates a short survey for use during the focus group sessions. Such a document can help to orient participants to the topic and can provide a filler task for those who arrive early. During this preparing stage, the facilitator identifies a time and arranges a specific location for the focus group meeting. Next, the facilitator selects and recruits members of the target population to participate in the focus group. Finally, the facilitator gathers resources for the session (for example, note paper, name tags, and flip-chart paper). In most cases, the facilitator also arranges refreshments for the participants.

Conduct

At the beginning of a session, the facilitator introduces himself or herself, identifies the purpose of the session, describes the facilitator role, establishes the objectives, reviews the agenda, and sets the ground rules. In some cases, a colleague can act as a recorder for the session; the facilitator should introduce this person and his or her role.

During the session, the facilitator must balance the following tasks:

- Lead and facilitate the discussion.
- Encourage participation.
- Manage those who dominate the discussion.
- Write responses on a flip chart.
- Ensure that the tape recorder (if used) is functioning (or have the recorder do this).
- Keep track of time so that the session ends as scheduled.

Report

The last phase in administering a focus group consists of two steps: analyzing data and preparing a report. The analysis of focus group data must be systematic, because all the reported findings must be supported by data (Krueger & Casey, 2000). Figure 3.5 shows various kinds of reports.

Chapter Eight contains additional information on how to report needs assessment results.

- Narrative reports are written, about 15 to 30 pages long, and include quotations.
- Top-line reports are written and often used for interim reports that are given to the client within several days of the focus group; they are several pages long and provide bullet points of information relevant to the purpose of the focus group.
- Bulleted reports are written and outline a narrative report using words and phrases that convey the report's meaning.
- Oral reports are verbal, tell the audience why the focus group was important, present findings, and allow the audience to respond to the results and ask questions.
- Electronic reports, which may be integrated into other types of reports, rely on Internet, data storage devices, and digital recording devices.

FIGURE 3.5 *Various Types of Focus Group Reports*

Surveys

Developing good surveys is difficult. Following a systematic process helps to ensure that the objectives and desired results are achieved. The phases involved in surveying needs are as follows:

- Prepare.
- Design.
- Develop questions.
- Write instructions.
- Write the cover letter.
- Pilot-test.
- Conduct the survey and follow-up.

Prepare

Critical tasks during the preparatory phase are to establish the goals for this data-collection effort and to become familiar with the situation and typical expressions. Before constructing a survey, it is useful to familiarize yourself with difficult terms. If necessary, consider using a subject-matter expert or an internal team member to translate technical jargon into simpler language.

You may also want to observe people in their work environments or review written reports. Observations can provide useful information about how people perform their job tasks, and conducting a few interviews can also help to surface items for the survey. Previous surveys and reports can provide figures, indices, or trends that help in framing specific questions. They may also provide question items that you can use in your survey.

At this point you will need to decide whether a previously designed or commercially available survey can be used or modified or whether you will need to design a new survey that is appropriate for the specific situation. The first two options may save you both time and money, but a survey specific to the particular issues, audience, or situation may not be available.

Design
When designing a survey, consider the following factors:

- *The number of people involved.* If the group to be surveyed is large, use mostly closed-ended questions that can be recorded and analyzed easily by computer. (More detail about closed-ended questions is provided later in this chapter.) If qualitative information is required, decide whether to include open-ended questions or conduct separate interviews or focus groups to collect the required information.
- *How the data will be collected.* Survey data may be collected using paper forms, or you may collect data by posting the survey online using an organization's intranet or the Internet.

Tip

Many online tools and services are available for creating surveys and collecting survey data. To find free tools and services, search the Internet using the term *free online survey*.

• *How the data will be analyzed.* Responses to online surveys are often analyzed with easy-to-use Web-based software. Responses to paper instruments can be analyzed by hand counting answers, or the surveys can be electronically scanned. Surveys that will be electronically scanned may require special predesigned "bubble" forms. In such cases, consider using the services of an internal market research department or an external agency to provide assistance in instrument design. Universities with data-processing departments may provide such services for a nominal fee.

• *Whether color schemes will be used.* Robinson and Robinson (1989) suggested using a color-coding system if a large number of surveys will be sent to different sources. This technique facilitates the data-analysis process by allowing completed surveys to be categorized by group for later analysis. If color papers are used, be sure they are pastel so that the print can be easily read.

Develop Questions

Nothing is more frustrating than sending out five hundred surveys to find out later that 60 percent of the respondents misinterpreted a question. When developing survey questions, it is crucial to follow a few basic guidelines.

Sequence questions. The sequence in which questions appear is important. It is generally effective to begin a survey with a few simple and interesting questions. Potentially sensitive questions should be presented later. In most cases, place demographic items at the end of the survey. Also, avoid clustering similar items together as well as labeling sections. Such clustering and labeling can create "halo" effects, which occur when the rating on an item affects the rating on another item.

Limit the amount of information gathered in one question. Requests for multiple pieces of information should always be divided into separate questions. For example, "Is this task challenging and rewarding?" asks for two pieces of information. In many cases, respondents will either overlook the second portion of the question entirely or just not answer it. A more effective way to gather the same information is to ask two questions, "Is this task challenging?" and "Is this task rewarding?"

Avoid complexity. Frame questions so they can be answered easily. Avoid asking questions that require extensive calculations. For example, "How many sales calls do you make in a year?" requires respondents to compute an annual figure based on their weekly or monthly totals. Similar information could be elicited by an easier question, "How many sales calls do you make per week?" or alternatively, "How many sales calls do you make in a typical work day?"

Word questions carefully. Questions must be clear and easy to understand. Here are a few guidelines to follow when wording questions:

- Use simple words.
- Avoid leading questions such as, "Do you feel that offering this well-tested management training program will improve your managerial skills?"
- Avoid negatively phrased questions such as, "Did you not receive the computer training?"

Determine the type of questions. As mentioned earlier, there are different types of questions. Two basic types are open-ended questions and closed-ended questions.

Open-ended questions require respondents to answer in their own words. Asking open-ended questions may elicit in-depth responses. For example, an open-ended question could be, "What do you see as the mission of this organization?"

Fill-in-the-blank questions, which represent a type of open-ended item, are useful when you want to limit the length of responses but are unable to determine all of the possible options. For example: "Your location: _____."

Asking open-ended or fill-in-the-blank questions is relatively easy. However, you should think carefully about using such questions in a survey because analyzing the various responses requires more time and effort than analyzing closed-ended questions.

Closed-ended questions, in contrast to open-ended questions, allow respondents to choose from defined options. An advantage to asking closed-ended questions is that they facilitate data entry and analysis. A disadvantage of asking closed-ended questions is that respondents cannot elaborate on their answers. There are several types of closed-ended questions:

- Two choice

- Multiple choice

- Scales of various kinds

Two-choice questions (for example, yes/no or true/false) are asked when an answer can be either one thing or the other, and the responses are mutually exclusive. For example:

Q. Everyone has access to the organization's mission statement.

    _____ True
    _____ False

Note that even with two-choice questions you must decide whether to provide other options, such as "don't know" or "not applicable."

Multiple-choice questions usually include a list of four or more options from which respondents select one or more responses. For example:

Q. With which of the following departments do you work most closely? (Check only one.)

    _____ a. Accounting
    _____ b. Information Services
    _____ c. Human Resources
    _____ d. Marketing
    _____ e. Operations

A fill-in-the-blank option may be included. The preceding example could offer an additional choice:

    _____ f. Other, please specify: _____

Scales of various kinds. Two types of scales commonly used in surveys are the Likert-type scale and the interval scale.

Survey items that ask respondents to rank or rate values and attitudes use *Likert-type scales* (Likert, 1932). When using such scales, it is usually best to assign the most positive value at the higher end of the scale (Paul & Bracken, 1995). Two examples follow:

Q. Employees should receive monthly safety training. (Check one of the following.)

> 1 = Strongly disagree
> 2 = Disagree
> 3 = Somewhat agree
> 4 = Agree
> 5 = Strongly agree

Q. How skilled are your coworkers in troubleshooting the new computer equipment? (Check one of the following.)

> 1 = Very low skilled
> 2 = Low skilled
> 3 = Average skilled
> 4 = Highly skilled
> 5 = Very highly skilled

Survey items that collect numeric information from or about respondents use *interval scales.* These scales are also useful for obtaining information about a range of possibilities. For example:

Q. How many loans do you close in a week? (Select one.)

> _____ a. Under 25
> _____ b. 25–35
> _____ c. 36–45
> _____ d. 46–55
> _____ e. Over 55

Note that a common mistake when creating interval scales is to provide options that overlap. Such a mistake would appear if we were to present the following option for the previous question:

Q. How many loans do you close in a week? (Circle only one.)

    a. Under 25
    b. 25–35
    c. 35–45
    d. 45–55
    e. 55 and over

[The respondent would have difficulty answering if the number of loans equaled 35, 45, or 55.]

Figure 3.6 summarizes when to use each type of question.

Write Instructions

The fourth phase in preparing surveys involves writing explicit instructions. When writing instructions, specify how respondents should complete the form. Explain whether they should circle items, use check marks, fill in the "bubble," or write comments. Indicate whether survey items require only one response or multiple responses. State the amount of time required to complete the survey, to whom it should be returned, and by when.

Write the Cover Letter

Another critical phase in implementing surveys is preparing the cover letter. A cover letter explains why the person is being asked to complete the survey and how they will benefit from it. To improve the response rate, ask a senior staff member (such as the president of the company) to endorse the survey with his or her signature. State whether the information that is gathered will be kept confidential.

Type of Question	When to Use the Question
Open-Ended or Fill-in-the-Blank	Obtain qualitative information
	Capture respondents' own words
	Probe for more information
	Seek more information as a follow-up to a closed-ended question
Closed-Ended	Obtain quantitative information
Two-Choice	Obtain opposite or mutually exclusive answers
Multiple Choice	Obtain one response from a list of choices (with instruction to "check only one")
	Obtain multiple responses from a list of choices (with instruction to "check as many as apply")
	Obtain responses with no rank order
	Obtain certain demographic data
Likert Scale	Obtain ratings (and possibly rank order)
Interval Scale	Obtain interval-level data
	Obtain certain demographic data

FIGURE 3.6 *Types of Questions and When to Use Them*

Pilot-Test

After a survey has been designed, it is usually a good idea to pilot-test it. A pilot test can identify problems in construction or physical layout; it can also answer the following questions:

- Are the instructions clear and concise?
- Can respondents understand the questions easily?
- Can respondents answer the questions easily?
- Do respondents have enough space to record their comments?
- Do the questions elicit responses that address the survey purpose?

The process of pilot-testing consists of several steps. If diverse groups will be surveyed, select a few people from each group. In a private meeting room, distribute the form and ask respondents to complete it while you are in the room. Observe the respondents' reactions closely and watch faces for reactions that may indicate confusion or frustration. In addition, ask respondents to write on the survey anything they found confusing. After the survey questions are answered, ask respondents to describe their understanding of each question, discuss their reasons for their responses, and identify any problems.

Later, summarize the results of the pilot test. Tabulate the pilot-test survey responses to see if there will be any problems with data analysis and if the kind of data produced addresses the purpose for the survey.

After an initial pilot test, make appropriate changes to the form and conduct a second pilot test. If the group size for the survey is more than two hundred people, use ten to twenty respondents in the pilot test (Callahan, 1985).

Tip

You may discover while analyzing pilot data that the survey responses do not really address the initial purpose of the survey. To save the day, revise the survey and pilot-test it again.

Conduct the Survey and Follow-Up

Upon completion of the pilot test, the survey is ready to launch. If a paper survey is used, print it on high-quality paper. If an online survey is used, launch the Web site. Be sure to monitor the incoming responses frequently. If you encounter nonrespondents—a situation that is very likely—be prepared to follow up (Dillman, 2000). The follow-up process involves sending a reminder three weeks after the initial survey was launched. Three weeks after that reminder, another copy of the survey is sent to all nonrespondents (if you know who the nonrespondents are) with a request to complete the survey as soon as possible; if you do not know who the nonrespondents are, you should send a copy of the survey to everyone, asking those who have not yet responded to complete the survey and return it.

Figure 3.7 summarizes the phases and steps for developing and implementing surveys. It also provides some additional tips.

Observation

Observation is another method used to collect data during needs assessments. When used systematically, observation can yield meaningful results. Like interview data, observational data can be collected in a structured or unstructured fashion. The time frame for the observation, whether structured or unstructured, is established. With structured observations, decisions as to exactly which factors will be monitored are made prior to the observation. For example, an analyst could use structured observation to monitor the number of employees in a kitchen who wash their hands prior to preparing food. With unstructured observations, the analyst collects information on all aspects of interest in a situation. For example, the analyst could observe the same kitchen to see and record all behaviors of interest.

Structured observations have some advantages:

- They reduce the potential for bias.
- They increase the reliability of observations.
- They provide an accurate way to report data.

As Rossett (1987) suggested, use the unstructured method to obtain an initial feel for a situation. Then follow up with a structured observation.

One problem that arises with observation, whether structured or unstructured, is that people often alter their behavior when being watched by others. To avoid this problem, use unobtrusive techniques. For example, observe people from an inconspicuous spot. You can reduce anxiety by dressing in attire similar to the attire of those you are observing.

1. Prepare.
- Familiarize yourself with the background situation.
- Speak with appropriate groups of employees to define and clarify jargon or technical terms.
- Establish the purpose and expected outcomes for the survey.

2. Design.
- Determine whether questions from previously developed surveys can be used in their entirety or in part.
- Determine whether any commercial surveys can be customized.
- Determine how confidentiality will be maintained.
- Consult with a technical specialist if an electronic or Web-based survey will be used or if computerized analysis will be performed.
- Determine how results will be analyzed and presented.
- Determine whether outsourcing will be necessary.
- Decide whether color schemes should be used.

3. Develop questions.
- Ensure that each question has a purpose.
- Determine which type of question (open- or closed-ended) will elicit the best response. (Limit the number of open-ended questions if the survey will be sent to a large number of people, to avoid needing an undue amount of time for data analysis.)
- Ensure that each question asks for only one piece of information.
- Avoid leading and biased questions.
- Avoid negatively phrased questions.
- Avoid personal or identifying questions.
- Ask questions that the respondents are qualified to answer.
- Avoid jargon, abbreviations, or colloquialisms.
- Use gender-neutral terms.
- Write questions that are clear and concise.
- Arrange questions in a logical sequence from general to specific.
- Position difficult or sensitive questions at the end.
- Number items.
- Provide space for comments.
- Use boldface or italic type and underline where appropriate.
- Use plenty of white space.
- Number pages.

4. Write instructions.
- Write instructions on how to answer questions.
- Explain complicated or confusing terms.

FIGURE 3.7 *Tips for Preparing and Implementing Surveys*

5. Write a cover letter.
- State the purpose of the survey.
- Provide a history of previous research or findings when appropriate.
- Show the benefit to the user.
- Explain why the respondent was selected.
- State when and how the form should be returned.
- Thank the respondent for completing the survey.

6. Pilot-test survey.
- Select participants for the pilot test.
- Conduct and observe the pilot test.
- Make appropriate modifications based on results of the pilot test.
- Conduct a second pilot test if necessary.
- Make final modifications.

7. Conduct the survey and follow-up.
- Distribute or post the survey.
- Determine the response rate.
- Send reminder memo, postcard, or e-mail three weeks following the original survey.
- Send a reminder and second survey three weeks following the first reminder.

FIGURE 3.7 *Tips for Preparing and Implementing Surveys* (continued)

The notes that document unstructured observation are usually recorded on notepaper or in a computer file that is labeled with the name of the observer, the location, and time of the observation. Forms are usually created to document structured observations. Here are a few tips for preparing structured observation forms:

- Include the name of the observer and the observation date and location.

- Include a checklist of items to be observed, including the individual tasks and subtasks performed during your observation and either the frequency of performance or the amount of time taken to perform a task. Also include the start and end times.

- Design the checklist with space for recording both qualitative and quantitative data.

- Provide space for comments and additional notes.

Documents and Artifacts

Another vital source of information in needs assessments are the data contained in current and historical documents and other artifacts such as business plans, mission statements, job descriptions, performance reviews, Web sites, training evaluation forms, sales records, customer-service call records, personnel records, budgets, and photographs. Such data can be qualitative or quantitative. The benefit of collecting such data is optimized when these data are collected in conjunction with another data-gathering method.

Following are a few tips for using data from documents and artifacts:

- Be clear about the type of information you are seeking before undertaking an extensive search of records.

- Seek permission prior to using archival or company records.

- Look for trends and patterns in the data.

Figure 3.8 summarizes the primary data-gathering methods discussed in this chapter.

TECHNOLOGY AND DATA COLLECTION

Given the wide use of technology today, you should consider incorporating technology into the data-collection process. As described by Gayeski (2004), wireless mobile technologies can be used effectively and efficiently to diagnose and solve performance problems. "The market is full of small, but powerful, PDAs [personal digital assistants] with digital cameras and audio plug-ins that can record interviews and other audio. You could take notes, quickly assemble a job aid that documented the repair, and wirelessly post it to a Website" (p. 49).

As another example, a survey can be administered in-person to a large or small audience using response technology. With response technology,

Method	When to Use	Time Required		Cost	Resources Required	
		Conduct or Implement	Analyze Data		HRD	Management
One-on-One Interviews	Conduct strategic, competency, job task analysis, or knowledge and skills assessment. Obtain sensitive information. Discuss complex issues that require explanations. Gain support.	High	High	Medium to high	Time Skilled interviewer	Budget Time
Phone Interviews	Conduct strategic or knowledge and skills assessment. Gather small pieces of information. Ask follow-up questions. Obtain information when respondents are geographically disbursed. Obtain information from many sources quickly. Obtain nonsensitive information. Obtain more quantifiable and qualitative information. Save travel costs.	Low to medium	Medium	Low	Time Skilled interviewer	Time

Focus Groups	Conduct strategic, competency, job task analysis, or knowledge and skills assessment. Collect qualitative data. Gather information when group behavior determines job performance.	Low	High	Medium to high	Time Skilled facilitator Note taker or recorder Budget
Surveys	Conduct strategic, competency, job task analysis, or knowledge and skills assessment. Use when individuals are geographically disbursed. Obtain quantifiable data. Responses to closed-ended questions can be categorized easily.	Low to medium	Low	Low	Time Knowledge of survey development Data tracking skills Data analysis skills Budget Administrative support

FIGURE 3.8 *Comparison of Primary Data-Gathering Methods*

Method	When to Use	Time Required		Cost	Resources Required	
		Conduct or Implement	Analyze Data		HRD	Management
Observations	Conduct strategic, job and task analysis, or knowledge and skills assessment. Document performance. Observe frequency of performance. Document amount of time taken to perform a task.	Low	Low to medium	Low	Time Availability of individuals Knowledge of the performance to be observed Observation form	
Current and Historical Documents and Other Artifacts	Conduct strategic, competency, job task analysis, or knowledge and skills assessment. Provide background information. Collect qualitative or quantitative data.	Low	Medium	Low	Time	Permission

FIGURE 3.8 *Comparison of Primary Data-Gathering Methods* (continued)

the survey participants use remote controllers to respond to each survey item as it appears via a PowerPoint presentation. The individual responses to each item are sent immediately to the analyst, who with the press of a button can show the group their collective responses and create a report.

Finally, it is important to recognize the usefulness of Web-based surveys. Respondents can access a survey and respond when it is convenient for them. Furthermore, the data are immediately captured in a database that can be easily analyzed.

Which technologies are useful will depend on the organization and the client. Consider how available technologies might be used effectively and efficiently for your situation.

DATA ANALYSIS

There are two kinds of data: quantitative and qualitative. Numerical data are *quantitative*. All other kinds of data are *qualitative*. Examples of quantitative data include sales records, product ratings, and time logs. Examples of qualitative data include words, graphics, videos, photographs, and sound recordings.

Quantitative data can be gathered, scored, and analyzed more easily and quickly than qualitative data. They may be summarized and presented using various kinds of tables, charts, and graphs. In contrast, qualitative data are more difficult and time-consuming to collect and analyze, but they provide rich and detailed information.

The computer software for analyzing quantitative data (such as Excel, SPSS, and SAS) or qualitative data (such as NVIVO and Atlas) improves the ease, accuracy, and speed of data analysis. The following paragraphs provide an overview of some of the basic analyses that can be used. More detailed and complex analyses are beyond the scope of this book. However, many books and articles describe specific procedures for analyzing various kinds of quantitative and qualitative data, and Chapter Ten contains references that will get you started.

Analyzing Quantitative Data

In most needs assessments, quantitative data analyses are limited to *descriptive statistics*. These analyses basically describe the survey data. Statistical software, such as SAS and SPSS, make it easy to do these calculations. However, you can also perform these calculations yourself.

To begin analyzing quantitative data, create a spreadsheet that includes all the items for which such data were collected. Figure 3.9 shows an example of such a tally sheet for analyzing the quantitative data obtained from a survey question. Of course you could create a similar tally sheet for quantitative data obtained through other methods (such as observations and interviews). The example shows the response choices for the item (such as extremely well, very well, and moderately well), the value of each response choice (for instance, 5 for extremely well), the frequency of each response (obtained by counting the actual responses), and the percentage of individuals who selected each response. Using this example, let us review how to calculate frequencies and percentages.

Frequency. This measure counts the number of times each response choice was selected. A quick glance at the frequency column in Figure 3.9 reveals that the greatest number of people (fifty-four) thought line workers performed the new process moderately well, but only five people thought line workers performed the new process extremely well.

Item	Response	Frequency	Percentage
How well did line workers perform the new process?	5 Extremely well	5	3
	4 Very well	14	8
	3 Moderately well	54	32
	2 Not well	51	31
	1 Not at all well	33	20
	No response	10	6
Total		167	100

FIGURE 3.9 *Example of Frequency and Percentage Calculation for a Quantitative Question Showing All Responses*

Percentages. This measure is useful for comparing the categories of responses. To calculate the percentage for a response, divide its frequency by the total frequency. For example, the percentage for the response *extremely well* was calculated by dividing its frequency (5) by the total (167) and then rounding the number (or .02994 or 3 percent).

It should be noted that in the preceding example the nonrespondents are included in the calculation of the percentages. Another option would be to calculate the percentages based only on those who responded (with N = 157), but when doing so it would be important to include the frequency of nonrespondents (that is, 10) and to indicate the total number of respondents plus nonrespondents (that is, 167). Figure 3.10 displays these results. It should be noted that in this example the total percentage adds up to 99 because of rounding.

Other Useful Measures

In addition to reporting the frequencies and percentages for each category, you can also report a single value that provides information about what is typical for a question. This value is called a "measure of central tendency." There are three different measures of central tendency: (1) the mode, (2) the median, and (3) the mean or average.

The *mode* is simply the most frequent response. Let us take the last example presented. In this case, the mode, or most frequent response, is "3 moderately well."

Item	Response	Frequency	Percentage
How well did line workers perform the new process?	5 Extremely well	5	3
	4 Very well	14	9
	3 Moderately well	54	34
	2 Not well	51	32
	1 Not at all well	33	21
	No response (10)		
Total		157	99

FIGURE 3.10 *Example of Frequency and Percentage Calculation for a Quantitative Question Showing Only Respondents*

The *median* represents the middle-most point, or the point that would divide the distribution into the top 50 percent and the bottom 50 percent. If we again take the last example and add the percentages from the bottom of the scale (21 + 32), we see that 50 percent would fall into the category of "2 not well." This, then, is the median.

The *mean* is the average for the question. The steps for calculating the mean are as follows:

1. For each response, multiply the response value by the number of respondents. The calculations for the responses in Figure 3.10 are as follows:

Extremely well	5 × 5	= 25
Very well	14 × 4	= 56
Moderately well	54 × 3	= 162
Not well	51 × 2	= 102
Not at all well	33 × 1	= 33
		378

2. Add the products for all responses (in this case, 25 + 56 + 162 + 102 + 33 = 378) and divide this total by the number of respondents (that is, 378/157 = 2.4076). In the example in Figure 3.10, the mean or average is thus 2.41.

Finally, you can report on the values that indicate the degree of spread, or variation, in the data. These values are called a *measure of variability*. Again, there are three options: (1) the range, (2) the interquartile range, and (3) the standard deviation.

The *range* simply measures the difference between the highest and the lowest response. So, in the preceding example, the range would consist of the difference between "5 extremely well" (the highest response) and "1 not at all well" (the lowest response), or 5 – 1 = 4. This measure communicates that in this case the highest and lowest response options were chosen by one or more of the respondents.

The *interquartile range* is the difference between the value at the 75th percentile and the value at the 25th percentile. In the case above, the value at the 75th percentile is "3 moderately well" and the value at the 25th percentile is "2 not well." So the interquartile range would be 3 – 2 = 1.

The *standard deviation* measures how much an individual value varies from the mean. A low standard deviation means that the responses vary little from the mean; a high standard deviation means that the responses vary greatly from the mean. One major advantage of the standard deviation is that it provides information needed for more advanced statistics. We use statistics software or math calculators to compute standard deviations. For the example in Figure 3.10, the standard deviation equals 1.02.

Although most needs assessments rely primarily on the descriptive statistics just discussed, there are occasions when it is necessary to undertake other types of analyses. These may involve making inferences from a sample group to the entire population (using inferential statistics), examining relationships (using correlational analyses), focusing on predicting relationships (using regression analyses), or testing for significant differences among variables or groups. To learn more about these types of statistics, refer to an introductory or advanced text on statistics and research methods.

Analyzing Qualitative Data

Analyzing qualitative data involves classifying the data into categories. These categories may come from other sources (such as previous data-collection efforts) or they may be derived from the current data. Categories derived from the current data can be developed by reviewing the entire data set and determining the major themes, or they can be derived from the use of specific words or phrases.

In most needs assessment projects, qualitative data includes responses to open-ended questions; thus the analysis involves reading and rereading the responses to determine the meaning of the statements. Once the meaning of a statement has been determined, one can decide how to categorize the response. The following steps should be used when undertaking such analyses:

- Read and reread each statement.

- Make notes or underline important phrases.

- Develop codes, such as a name, acronym, or number, for each category.

- Assign codes to each statement and sort them into the categories.

- Review the statements within each category and revise the categorization.

- Have a colleague sort some of the data into the categories and compare the results with the earlier categorization of data to determine the level of agreement.

- Count the number of statements within each category.

- Decide how you will report the results.

For more complex qualitative analyses, please consult the resources in Chapter Ten.

Reliability, Validity, and Trustworthiness Related to Data Collection and Analysis

Reliability, validity, and *trustworthiness* are terms that describe the level of confidence we have in the data collection and analysis. *Reliability* refers to the degree of consistency. This consistency can be among raters (as with the agreement among different people categorizing qualitative data), among questions in a survey that measure the same concept, or among responses to similar surveys given at different times. Measures of reliability, such as Cronbach's alpha or test-retest reliability, can be calculated with most statistical software packages.

Validity refers to how well the data-collection method or instrument accurately reflects the concepts or phenomena being measured. For example, validity provides information about the extent to which a survey and the items it contains accurately measure employees' skills. To

> **Tip**
>
> You would probably not believe data that were collected using a rubber ruler. The data would not be reliable because the measurements would change depending on how taut the ruler was. Similarly, you should examine other data-collection instruments to determine whether they collect data consistently.

obtain face validity as well as some measure of content validity, have the data-collection methods reviewed by subject-matter experts. Other forms of validity require statistical analyses. More information on these analyses can be found in the resources appearing in Chapter Ten.

Trustworthiness is a concept closely related to reliability and validity but it tends to be used for qualitative data and qualitative analyses. Guba and Lincoln (1981)proposed four criteria for trustworthiness:

- *Truth value:* the degree to which one can establish the "truth" of the findings, potentially by using multiple methods

- *Applicability:* the degree to which the findings may be applicable in other settings

- *Consistency:* the degree to which the results can be considered reliable and stable

- *Neutrality:* the degree to which the findings come from the study and not from the biases of the analyst

Being attentive to the data-collection methods and analyses and determining the levels of reliability, validity, and trustworthiness provides support for the needs assessment findings. We can place more confidence in rigorously collected and analyzed data than in shoddily collected and analyzed data. Further details on these procedures can be found in Russ-Eft and Preskill (2001) and in the resources provided in Chapter Ten.

CONCLUSION

Data collection and analysis are essential parts of needs assessment. This chapter has described the most commonly used methods of data gathering. As seen, each method has its strengths and weaknesses. Needs assessments are optimized when a combination of data-gathering methods is used. This chapter also has described methods for analyzing quantitative and qualitative data. Regardless of which methods are used to collect and analyze data, it is important to consider the reliability, validity, and trustworthiness of the data.

The tools and concepts presented in this chapter will be used throughout the book. The next chapter describes how to collect and analyze data when conducting a knowledge and skills assessment.

II

Getting Down to Brass Tacks

FOUR Knowledge and Skills Assessment

PURPOSE

This chapter will enable you to accomplish the following:

- Determine what a knowledge and skills assessment is.

- Know when to use a knowledge and skills assessment.

- Recognize the benefits and drawbacks of the approach.

- Identify critical success factors for completing a knowledge and skills assessment.

- Examine the steps for undertaking a knowledge and skills assessment.

- Examine how a knowledge and skills assessment was conducted at Packaged Delivery, Inc.

RELATED TOOLKIT JOB AIDS

The following job aids are available in the Toolkit section of this book for use with the material in this chapter:

- Knowledge and Skills Assessment Interview Guide
- Skills Assessment Survey
- Customer-Service Knowledge and Skills Assessment Survey
- Management Knowledge and Skills Assessment Survey
- Knowledge and Skills Assessment Curriculum Plan

OVERVIEW

As a human performance generalist for a medium-sized manufacturing company, you may need to implement a company-wide orientation program; as the training manager of a large health care facility, you may be asked to develop a series of management training programs for supervisory staff; as the HRD manager within a global financial services organization, you may need to launch a sales development initiative; or as the learning specialist within an agency, you may be asked to create a cultural awareness program. Before launching any training, learning, or development program, you must usually gather information about the developmental needs of your target group or groups and determine whether training is, in fact, the appropriate solution.

By using a systematic approach, you can ensure that gaps in performance are identified correctly. Usually, only those gaps caused by lack of knowledge or skills can be improved through training. Performance deficiencies that occur because of lack of motivation, environmental problems, or systems issues require non-training interventions, such as changes in the selection process, the performance appraisal process, the reward system, or the production system.

When designing training programs, the roles of HRD and HPT professionals vary, but some of their more common responsibilities include the following:

- Creating a training agenda
- Developing a specific training program (course or module)

- Developing a training curriculum
- Implementing the agenda, program, or curriculum

A needs assessment provides the information that is necessary for designing and implementing effective training programs. The basic purpose of a knowledge and skills assessment is twofold:

1. To identify the knowledge and skills that people must possess in order to perform effectively on the job
2. To prescribe appropriate interventions that can close the knowledge and skills gaps

The amount of time spent conducting needs assessments varies. Although most knowledge and skills assessments are performed in less than a month, a few take up to a year or more to complete. The knowledge and skills assessment described in the case presented later in this chapter was completed in five weeks.

When to Use

A knowledge and skills assessment is most likely to be useful under the following circumstances:

- When new business opportunities arise
- When a new system or technology must be implemented
- When existing training programs must be revised or updated
- When new job responsibilities must be assumed by people
- When jobs must be upgraded
- When organizations undergo downsizing
- When organizations experience rapid growth

Benefits and Drawbacks

There are two main benefits from conducting a knowledge and skills assessment:

- It ensures that training programs are developed based on identified needs.

- It is relatively easy to implement.

The main drawback to the approach is that it lacks the detail of a job and task analysis, a competency assessment, or a strategic needs assessment. These more in-depth and complex assessment methods are described in Chapters Five, Six, and Seven.

Critical Success Factors

The following factors must be present for the successful completion of a knowledge and skills assessment:

- Support, both human and monetary, from senior officials or senior management as well as from the community members or line staff

- Buy-in from special interest groups, such as labor unions, especially if the assessment is perceived by some as a threat to their positions

- Availability of personnel for data-gathering purposes

KEY PHASES

A knowledge and skills assessment is made up of five phases:

Phase 1: Gather preliminary data

Phase 2: Plan

Phase 3: Perform training requirements analysis

1. Develop tools

2. Collect data

Phase 4: Analyze data

Phase 5: Prepare and present a report

Phase 1: Gather Preliminary Data

As mentioned earlier, deficiencies in human performance and changes in the environment often trigger the need for training. For instance, managers in Company A may be outstanding coaches but lack technical skills. Technical staff in Company B may not have problems operating machine X because they are familiar with the procedures, but they may have problems operating machine Y, which was recently installed. Community members may understand the need for collaboration, but lack the needed skills.

In any case, the first step in conducting a knowledge and skills assessment is to gather some preliminary information about the training or performance needs of the target groups. As a first step, review available documents and records. These may include statements about the organization's or unit's goals, performance data (such as production records, error rates, safety violations, and performance appraisal records), and training materials and records. (See Chapter Three for more details on reviewing records and documents.)

After the document review, some additional sources that can be tapped for conducting this preliminary analysis include the following:

- Senior officials and managers
- Target audience
- Functional heads or managers of the target audience
- Subordinates
- Internal or external customers

- Suppliers

- Others (such as peers or technical support staff)

Since you are gathering preliminary information, it is usually best to conduct these individual or group interviews with three to five people. This will enable you to obtain different perspectives without devoting large amounts of time to the task. If a key person is unavailable for a face-to-face interview, the same information may be obtained through a phone interview.

For a manufacturing company, the primary group could consist of a senior manager, a midlevel manager, a subordinate, and a relatively new employee. For a health care facility, information could be obtained from a senior manager, a first-line supervisor, and a subordinate. For a global financial services organization, interviews could be undertaken with the senior vice president of sales, the senior vice president of marketing, a regional sales manager, and a sales associate. For an international development organization, information could be obtained from a funding partner, a senior manager, and regional associates. As indicated in these examples, it is critical to obtain the perspectives of one or two key decision makers (such as senior managers).

The objectives of this phase are as follows:

1. *Establish the goals of the assessment.* As the following example illustrates, the goals expressed by various interviewees could be quite different from one another in purpose and scope. It is therefore critical to clarify the purpose of an assessment in the beginning so that appropriate data can be collected.

- Goal 1: Determine the worldwide knowledge and skills of all Company Y technicians.

- Goal 2: Determine the knowledge and skills of all Company Y Level 1 and Level 2 technicians in the United States and Canada.

2. *Obtain a holistic perspective about the knowledge and skills.* In particular, it is important to determine whether the solution really should involve training or should focus on some other systemic issues. (See McLean, 2005, for some ideas about addressing non-training issues.) Use the general questions in Toolkit Form 4.1 to help elicit a broad understanding about whether and how a lack of knowledge and skills is affecting workplace productivity. The second set of questions on the form can be used to develop a better understanding with the client about what the needs assessment should accomplish. After all the necessary data have been obtained, summarize your findings in a brief report that contains the following elements:

- Statement of the problem
- Situation analysis
- Goals
- Preliminary findings
- Next steps

An example of a report that outlines the context for one knowledge and skills assessment is given on pages 84–85. This information was provided by Julie Suchanek, government relations director for the Oregon Community College Association's Legislative Committee.

Phase 2: Plan

The next step involves developing a work plan to ensure that you stay on target with your assessment. Sometimes this work plan is developed as part of a larger proposal, as discussed in Chapter Eight. When preparing a work plan, seek the input of your client or contact at the beginning of the project, because this person usually has the best knowledge of group operations, peak business periods to avoid, and so forth. The four steps for planning an assessment begin on page 85.

STATEMENT OF THE PROBLEM

The Oregon Community College Association (OCCA) Legislative Committee comprises seventeen members—the institutional president or a local board member from each Oregon community college. Beyond attendance at the committee meetings, the rate by which committee members are retaining information, taking action on the information retained, and developing leadership in the area of the legislature is unclear.

SITUATION ANALYSIS

The charge to the committee is to recommend legislative and policy actions to the thirty-four-member OCCA board. These recommendations shape the positions the OCCA takes on policies before the Oregon legislature and various commissions and boards at the state level.

GOALS

The purpose of assessing the needs of the OCCA Legislative Committee is to determine the level of learning and involvement by members of the committee. The assessment focuses on three criteria—member morale, member engagement, and member action—to uncover the level of respect for the committee perceived by committee members, information retained by members, and how this translates into legislative action by members.

PRELIMINARY FINDINGS

Observation and selected interviews indicate that there may be varying levels of member morale, member engagement, and member action.

NEXT STEPS

Further data collection will involve additional observations and review of available documents and records. A knowledge and skills assessment will be undertaken with all committee members. By identifying how the committee is perceived by its own members, OCCA can work to increase learning in an effort to increase morale, engagement, and action by committee members.

1. *Determine what types of data must be collected.* The goals established in the first needs assessment phase set the stage for data-collection efforts in this phase.

2. *Determine sources of data.* For groups with fewer than thirty members, include every person in your study. If your target audience includes different groups or hierarchical levels, select a representative sample from each group or level. For more information on sample sizes, consult *Performance Consulting* by Robinson and Robinson (1995) or *Evaluation in Organizations* by Russ-Eft and Preskill (2001). In addition, use the following guidelines when making decisions about whom to include in an assessment:

- When implementing a new system or technology, involve technical or subject-matter experts, the target audience, supervisors, and end users.

- When assessing knowledge and skill needs for an existing process, involve subject-matter experts, job incumbents, supervisors, and other related internal or external customers.

- When revising or updating an existing training program or an HRD or HPT intervention, include the target audience and supervisors. Consider including subject-matter experts and other related internal or external customers if needed or required.

- When developing a new training program or an HRD or HPT intervention, include the target audience, subject-matter experts (if required), supervisors, and other related internal or external customers.

3. *Examine the purposes of the knowledge and skills assessment and determine the types of analyses that must be performed.* Figure 4.1 shows some of the common purposes of a knowledge and skills assessment and suggests the kinds of questions that will be addressed by the analyses. Usually, the specific business needs of an organization will determine whether any statistical analyses, such as correlations, must be computed. As mentioned in Chapter Three, if you lack expertise in such areas as statistics or survey design, consider engaging someone with expertise in preparing data-collection instruments and in analyzing data.

4. *Identify the types of tools that will be used to collect data.* Typically, using two or three different data-gathering methods increases the valid-

---

1. Learner analysis (What do learners know or need to know, and what do they not know?)
2. Subject-matter analysis (What do subject-matter experts say is important?)
3. Comparison of knowledge levels: current versus desired (How does the current level of knowledge differ from what is needed or desired?)
4. Comparison of skill levels: current versus desired (What are the current skills and how do they differ from what is needed or desired?)
5. Attitude toward learning (What is the attitude toward learning among the target group?)
6. Attitude toward change (What is the attitude toward change among the target group?)
7. Attitude toward existing training programs (What is the attitude about the current training programs?)
8. Attitude toward a new system or technology (What is the attitude toward the new system or technology?)
9. Quality of existing training programs (What is the quality level of the existing training programs?)

FIGURE 4.1 *Common Purposes of a Knowledge and Skills Assessment*

ity, trustworthiness, and reliability of data. For instance, you could supplement surveys with follow-up interviews or observations, or you could use focus groups as your primary data-gathering tool and collect additional information through observation. An overview of the primary data-gathering methods, including their benefits and drawbacks, is given in Chapter Three.

After you have completed the four steps of Phase 2, inform the people involved about your plan through letters, phone calls, or e-mail, and obtain approval from the client and advisory group to proceed with the assessment.

Phase 3: Perform Training Requirements Analysis

A performance gap is the difference between the current condition (or what is), and the desired condition (or what should be). A knowledge and skills assessment helps to define such a gap by identifying where performance deficiencies exist. The first two phases helped to lay the groundwork for developing the assessment instruments or tools. The third phase consists of two steps: develop the assessment tools and collect the assessment data.

Step 1: Develop Assessment Tools

Because every organization's assessment requirements are unique, the best strategy is to follow the basic guidelines for preparing interview forms, surveys, and focus group questions discussed in Chapter Three. As a guideline, allow about two days to prepare each instrument, but be prepared to allow additional time if special features must be included.

Figures 4.2 and 4.3 are examples of instruments for measuring gaps in skill proficiencies. Figure 4.2 is a simple self-assessment instrument that was used to monitor job activity levels at a major hospital. Figure 4.3 shows a portion of a performance skills profile for assessing the knowledge and skills of employees at an insurance company. A blank form that can be customized is provided in the Toolkit section at the back of the book (see Toolkit Form 4.2).

Instructions: For each task activity, circle the number corresponding to its importance for your job, the amount of time you spend on it, and how well you feel you perform it.

	Importance	Amount of Time Spent	Performance
Importance scale	1 – Unimportant; 2 – Minor; 3 – Important; 4 – Very Important; 5 – Critical		
Amount of Time Spent scale		0 – Never do this task; 1 – Very little compared to other tasks; 2 – Somewhat less compared to other tasks; 3 – Same amount as other tasks; 4 – More compared to other tasks; 5 – A great deal more compared to other tasks	
Performance scale			1 – Have low or no skill; 2 – Perform well enough to get by; 3 – Perform in this area without any problem; 4 – Have a definite strength or high skill; 5 – Have maximum skill

Medicare Tape Run

Task	Importance	Amount of Time Spent	Performance
Edit Lists	1 2 3 4 5	0 1 2 3 4 5	1 2 3 4 5
Tape List Claims	1 2 3 4 5	0 1 2 3 4 5	1 2 3 4 5
Paper Claims	1 2 3 4 5	0 1 2 3 4 5	1 2 3 4 5
Sort Error Claims for Reviewers	1 2 3 4 5	0 1 2 3 4 5	1 2 3 4 5
Call on Medicare Tape Runs	1 2 3 4 5	0 1 2 3 4 5	1 2 3 4 5
Work All Railroad EOB's	1 2 3 4 5	0 1 2 3 4 5	1 2 3 4 5
Check All Payments	1 2 3 4 5	0 1 2 3 4 5	1 2 3 4 5
Review All Rejects	1 2 3 4 5	0 1 2 3 4 5	1 2 3 4 5
Resubmit with Correct Information	1 2 3 4 5	0 1 2 3 4 5	1 2 3 4 5
Meet with Supervisor for Major Problems	1 2 3 4 5	0 1 2 3 4 5	1 2 3 4 5
Work on Groups	1 2 3 4 5	0 1 2 3 4 5	1 2 3 4 5
Call Patients to Correct Primary Insurance	1 2 3 4 5	0 1 2 3 4 5	1 2 3 4 5
Call Medicare to Update Insurance	1 2 3 4 5	0 1 2 3 4 5	1 2 3 4 5

FIGURE 4.2 *Job Activity Self-Assessment*

1. About You

Name: _____ Date: _____

a. Department: _____ Date of Employment: _____

Title of Current Job: _____

Objective of Current Job *(Describe in ten words or less.):* _____

_____

b. What equipment do you routinely use in your current work? *(Check all that apply.)*

____ Telephone ____ Computer (terminal) ____ PC

____ Typewriter ____ Calculator ____ Fax ____ Copier

____ Microphone ____ Other

c. List other equipment here:

_____

_____

2. About Your Formal Education *(optional)*

Circle the highest scholastic level achieved: 11 or below, 12, 13,
                                              14, 15, 16, 17, 18, 19, or more

3. About Your Work Experience

a. What *other* positions have you held? *(List most current first.)*

Title   Brief Description of Job Objective

_____

_____

_____

_____

_____

b. Equipment used in these jobs *(other than those listed above)*

_____

_____

4. About Your Computer Experience

Listed below are some of the most common computer applications used at our company.

In column A, rate your skill level in the application used in your current job.

In column B, rate your skill level in the application not used in your current job but in which you possess prior experience.

FIGURE 4.3 *Performance Skills Profile*

If an item is not applicable, place a check mark in the NA column.
Use the following scale:

None	Poor	Average	Good	Excellent
1	2	3	4	5

A   B   NA

			Item	Description
___	___	___	Active Directory	User interface
___	___	___	CMW	Medical billing system
___	___	___	Dragon Naturally Speaking	Voice-activated system
___	___	___	EMR	Electronic medical records
___	___	___	End Notes	Notes and citation system
___	___	___	HTML	Hypertext markup language
___	___	___	Lotus Notes	E-mail and forms
___	___	___	Microsoft Office	MS Office applications, as follows:
___	___	___	Access	Database
___	___	___	Excel	Spreadsheet
___	___	___	Outlook	Calendar and e-mail
___	___	___	PowerPoint	Presentation
___	___	___	Project	Project management
___	___	___	Publisher	Publication
___	___	___	Visio	Flow charts, process, and so on
___	___	___	Word	Word processor
___	___	___	MS Visual Studio	Programming
___	___	___	Netware Utilities	Novell application
___	___	___	Windows	User interface
___	___	___	WordPerfect	Word processor
___	___	___	XML	Markup language

Please add below and rate those applications not listed above.

___ ___ _____

___ ___ _____

___ ___ _____

5. About Training Related to Your Occupation
List below any formal training received *during the last five years* relating to any job you held at *any company*. List in sequence beginning with the most current.

FIGURE 4.3 *Performance Skills Profile* (continued)

Date	Name of Training Course	Date	Name of Training Course

1. _____   5. _____
2. _____   6. _____
3. _____   7. _____
4. _____   8. _____

(If you need more space, use a separate sheet and print your name on it.)

6. **About Assessing Your Training Needs**

 Given your current duties, accountabilities, and position objectives, assign two ratings to each of the items listed below.

 In column A, rate *your need* for training.

 In column B, rate *its importance* to your job.

 If an item is *not applicable,* place a check mark in the NA column.

 Provide a rating, as above, for any entry you make on the "other" line.

 Use the following scale:

Very low	Low	Average	High	Very high
1	2	3	4	5

A   B   NA   *Communication Skills*

___ ___ ___   **a.** Oral communication skills

___ ___ ___   **b.** Written communication skills (letters/memos/reports)

___ ___ ___   **c.** Formal presentation skills

___ ___ ___   **d.** Leading effective meetings

___ ___ ___   **e.** Other. Please specify: _____

Customer-Service Skills

___ ___ ___   **a.** Telephone skills

___ ___ ___   **b.** Listening/questioning skills

___ ___ ___   **c.** Handling difficult customers and complaints

___ ___ ___   **d.** Other. Please specify: _____

Performance Management Skills

___ ___ ___   **a.** Monitoring performance/correcting problems

___ ___ ___   **b.** Providing feedback/motivation

___ ___ ___   **c.** Coaching, counseling

___ ___ ___   **d.** Conflict management

___ ___ ___   **e.** Other. Please specify: _____

FIGURE 4.3 *Performance Skills Profile* (continued)

In addition, Toolkit Form 4.3, a customer-service training survey, and Toolkit Form 4.4, a management development survey, are included to help you start to develop these types of assessments. Note that Toolkit Form 4.4, the management development survey, can be administered to the managers' managers, their subordinates, or both to obtain many perspectives about managerial effectiveness in the organization. Following are some additional tips to consider when developing tools:

- Refer to the goals and objectives of your assessment.
- Include an opening paragraph (a statement of purpose and instructions for completing a survey, or an overview and introduction for interviews and focus groups), an indication of the confidentiality of the responses, the main section (the questions), and a closing (possibly demographic questions in the case of surveys, or closing remarks for conducting interviews or focus groups).
- Separate and label sections clearly.
- Include appropriate labels when using a rating scale.
- Decide whether to use an even-numbered rating scale, such as a four-point or six-point scale, or an odd-numbered scale, such as a five-point or seven-point scale. An odd-numbered scale allows respondents to choose the middle rating rather than be forced to choose one end of the scale or the other. Scales that have more points give respondents more choices, but, if the group is too small, make it difficult to see patterns in the data.
- If you use two sets of rating scales per question (shown below) and want to combine them, seek the expertise of someone who can interpret the results accurately. For example:

	PROFICIENCY				
	Very Low	Low	Average	High	Very High
Operate DVD	1	2	3	4	5

	IMPORTANCE TO JOB				
	Very Low	Low	Average	High	Very High
Operate DVD	1	2	3	4	5

- Limit the number of questions so that interviews and focus groups can be concluded in two and a half hours and surveys can be completed in twenty-five or thirty minutes.

- Limit the number of items to be assessed in a survey. For instance, if you listed more than fifty items and the majority received a rating of 3 or below (indicating that training is needed), you would need to develop a training plan that could accommodate all these programs. Because most people attend an average of seven training programs per year, it could take several years to train everyone. A more effective strategy is to prioritize the items to be included in a survey on the basis of the most critical requirements for the job.

- Pilot-test the data-collection instruments and revise them based on feedback.

Step 2: Collect Data

After you have prepared your instruments, you will be ready to begin the data-collection process. Here are a few tips to remember when collecting data:

- When working in a team, ensure that everyone follows the same procedure.

- Limit the time allowed for returning surveys, usually to ten days.

- Have supervisors or managers follow up if instruments have not been received after the ten-day limit.

Phase 4: Analyze Data

After completing Phase 3, you will have collected data from surveys, interviews, or focus groups. To analyze the data, use the process for compiling results that you selected for your plan in Phase 2. Following are a few strategies for ensuring success:

- Limit responsibility for this task: assume it yourself or delegate it to one or two individuals whose judgment and skills you trust.

- Review the data for discrepancies, deviations, and irregularities.

- Present irregularities in the data in a separate section.

- Always keep your client apprised of discrepancies in the data.

- Omit extraneous or irrelevant data; for example, eliminate facts or details that do not pertain specifically to the assessment and its objective. (This includes extraneous information that you may have gathered while interviewing or conducting focus groups.)

- List responses that do not fall into a previously defined category in a separate section titled "other."

- Establish codes for qualitative data (that is, data that are not numerical) so that you can group responses into categories. For example, review the responses to the open-ended survey questions to determine whether there are major themes or categories. If the majority of responses to a question fall into three main categories, assign codes A, B, or C (or relevant descriptive words) to the data according to the three predetermined categories. This coding scheme can then be used as you review the notes or tape-recordings from the interviews or focus groups. As you review the data, you may need to add additional categories that emerge.

- Next to each category, list the frequency of responses. For example:

Q. Why do you think team training is needed?

TYPE OF RESPONSE	NUMBER OF RESPONSES
A. People don't know how to work in teams.	15
B. There is lack of cooperation among units.	10
C. There is lack of clarity about team roles.	11

- When faced with conflicting data, seek the opinion of an expert or individual qualified to make a judgment.

Phase 5: Prepare and Present a Report

The final phase of a knowledge and skills assessment is preparing and presenting a formal report. Reports generally contain the following elements:

- Executive summary

- Goals or objectives

- Overview of data-collection methods

- Findings or conclusions

- Recommendations

- Appendix

Chapter Eight provides additional information on report writing. Other examples of formal reports can be found in Holton (1995).

Here are a few guidelines for presenting your conclusions and recommendations to your client and interested stakeholders:

- Tailor the presentation style to the culture of your organization.

- Verify budgetary constraints so that recommendations are on target.

- Present your recommendations in a table with the following headings: cost, urgency, availability of resources (monetary and non-monetary), and feasibility.

- Research the feasibility of each recommendation thoroughly and offer alternatives where needed.

- Use benchmarking data when available.

- Provide cost-benefit information, if appropriate.

- Support your recommendations with citations and "best practices" from authorities in the field or industry.

If you are preparing and presenting a curriculum plan, following is a suggested list of content areas to include:

- Overview
- Statement of the problem
- Learner analysis
- Detailed course objectives
- Course outlines
- Training schedule (quarterly, bi-annual, or annual)
- Training delivery strategy
- Evaluation strategy

Toolkit Form 4.5 can be used to develop high-level and detailed curriculum plans. The plan can include a core or advanced curriculum or both. Usually, core curriculums are more appropriate for beginning or intermediate learners.

This chapter has presented the methods and tools for performing a knowledge and skills assessment. Here is a case study of an assessment completed for Packaged Delivery, Inc.

The information for this case was contributed by Jeanne Strayer, a training and performance improvement consultant based in Oceanside, California. Although all events are real, the company has been given a fictitious name at the request of the contributor. The case shows the approach used to conduct a needs assessment in preparation for a new company-wide training program. The key tool shown here is a set of interview questions used for lead drivers, first-line supervisors, and senior managers.

Packaged Delivery, Inc., is one of the largest packaged product delivery companies in the United States. It manufactures and distributes products through home and commercial delivery, as well as through retail outlets such as supermarkets. The company has six regions in ten states. Each region has between four and six branches. Each branch is responsible for delivering its product to customers on designated routes. Depending on the size of the branch, lead drivers may report to two or more sales supervisors.

THE NEED

Packaged Delivery, Inc., recognized that lead drivers were being asked to expand their job duties. Because of their seniority, leads were expected to coach and train their peers—those responsible for driving routes and delivering products. The leads benefited because coaching offered a balance to their driving, delivery, and book-keeping duties. The company benefited because the leads often noticed and corrected performance problems with new trainees. Yet the leads did not necessarily have the skills to be effective trainers and coaches. Although they had sound technical skills, developing people required a different type of skill. The company saw the need for a program to help drivers learn to train and coach others.

THE APPROACH

A five-phase approach to conducting the needs assessment was used. The major steps and findings in each phase are summarized here.

Phase 1: Gather Preliminary Data

Preliminary data were gathered when the designated course developer met with the HR director and two regional vice presidents. The group confirmed the situation but also pointed out some unique characteristics of the leads' situation that had to be addressed:

- Leads were placed in a position of responsibility but had little or no authority.
- It was difficult for leads to find time to train and coach because their regular duties consumed so much time.
- Leads needed to strike the right balance between resolving problems behind the scenes and going to the supervisor when management intervention was required, which was especially true because of union regulations.
- Leads were often promoted within the same group, a situation that sometimes led to new dynamics and tensions with their former peers.

Phase 2: Develop a Plan

1. The HR director and two regional vice presidents agreed to the scope of the training and the plan for the needs assessment. All operational leads in the company (approximately 110 people) would be trained. The needs assessment would involve interviews with members of the target audience (the leads), their supervisors, and selected HR personnel who were seen as expert in coaching skills and union practices.

2. The following goals were identified for the interviews:

- Determine the gap between current and desired levels of training and coaching skills.
- Assess the leads' attitudes toward training.
- Obtain stories about real-life situations that could later serve as examples, case studies, or role-plays during the training.

Phase 3: Conduct a Needs Assessment

1. Interview instruments were created for the leads (see Figure 4.4), their supervisors (see Figure 4.5), and the company's vice presidents (see Figure 4.6).

2. Instruments were reviewed and approved by the HR director.

3. Interviews were conducted with fourteen leads, six supervisors, and two regional vice presidents. Interviews with the supervisors and vice presidents confirmed the data collected from the leads.

4. Interviews with HR personnel were particularly helpful in determining the types of coaching and training skills needed for nonsupervisory positions. These interviews also provided valuable insights into the constraints faced by the leads when working as union members.

Phase 4: Analyze the Data

1. Recurring themes in the qualitative interview data were noted, organized into categories, and coded. For example, responses to a question about obstacles to coaching others while working on the job were grouped into three categories:

-   Lack of time to coach
-   Physical environment (open spaces with no privacy)
-   Personal reluctance to coach former peers

2. The interviews also yielded quantitative, or numerical, data that helped to determine and rate the deficiencies in the leads' skills. The items and their ratings included the following (on a 5-point scale with 1 as low and 5 as high):

-   Listening empathetically 3.2
-   Giving directions clearly 3.2
-   Giving feedback constructively 3.0
-   Involving people rather than telling them what to do 2.5

1. According to the job description, a lead driver spends time training new hires and coaching experienced drivers as well as covering open routes. What percentage of your time do you estimate is spent on training and coaching?

2. What common performance problems do new hires have? Experienced drivers?

3. What sorts of situations call for coaching on your part?

4. What are the biggest challenges of a lead driver's job?

5. What were the biggest pitfalls you encountered as a new coach and trainer?

   Follow-up question #1: What mistakes did you make at first?

   Follow-up question #2: What lessons have you learned over time?

6. What do you do when someone is having trouble or not meeting standards?

7. Can you tell me about a successful experience you have had coaching someone?

   Follow-up question #1: What made it successful?

8. Tell me about a not-so-successful experience you have had coaching someone.

   Follow-up question #1: Why was it not successful?

9. How do you encourage and motivate other lead drivers?

   Follow-up question #1: Do you use incentives or rewards?

   Follow-up question #2: Do you try other things (for example, pay compliments, recognize people, give personal attention)?

10. What keeps you from being a good coach on the job?

11. Have you received training in coaching people?

12. Please rate yourself on the following skills on a scale of 1 (low) to 5 (high). These ratings are confidential and will not be attributed to any one person.

    a. Listening empathetically

    b. Giving directions clearly

    c. Giving feedback constructively

    d. Involving people rather than telling them what to do

    e. Demonstrating a new skill in such a way that another person understands the critical aspects, that is, does it correctly

    f. Guiding a team member to a solution for a problem

    g. Knowing how to recognize someone for a job well done

    h. Pointing out how someone's behavior is negatively affecting indicators and key measures

13. What topics would you like to see covered in training?

FIGURE 4.4 *Interview Questions for Lead Drivers*

1. According to the job description, a lead driver spends time training new hires and coaching experienced drivers, as well as covering open routes. What percentage of a driver's time do you estimate is spent doing training and coaching?
2. What are some of the skills you expect a lead driver to demonstrate as a coach or trainer?
   Follow-up question #1: Do the lead drivers currently perform these skills?
   Follow-up question #2: Why or why not?
3. What would the impact be on your branch if lead drivers were used effectively as coaches and trainers?
4. What kinds of situations call for coaching by drivers?
   Follow-up question #1: What measures should be taken?
5. What is a common performance problem for a new hire?
   Follow-up question #1: For an experienced driver?
6. What are the biggest challenges lead drivers face as coaches?
7. What are the biggest pitfalls you have seen new coaches fall into?
   Follow-up question #1: What mistakes do they commonly make?
8. Do lead drivers have the skills to help solve a problem rather than just bring it to the person's attention?
   Follow-up question #1: For example, can a lead driver come up with strategies to help someone increase sales, improve customer satisfaction ratings, and so on?
9. Think about the lead drivers who report to you now. How would you rate them on a scale of 1 (low) to 5 (high). These ratings are confidential and will not be attributed to any one person.
   a. Listening empathetically
   a. Listening empathetically
   b. Giving directions clearly
   c. Giving feedback constructively
   d. Involving people rather than telling them what to do
   e. Demonstrating a new skill in such a way that another person understands the critical aspects, that is, does it correctly
   f. Guiding a team member to a solution for a problem
   g. Knowing how to recognize someone for a job well done
   h. Pointing out how someone's behavior is negatively affecting indicators and key measures
   i. Encouraging and motivating others
10. Does anything keep lead drivers from being good coaches on the job?
    Follow-up question #1: Are there physical constraints, time constraints, or other factors?
11. Have lead drivers received any training in coaching people?
12. What topics would you like to see covered in training?

FIGURE 4.5 *Interview Questions for Supervisors*

---

1. How would you like to see lead drivers used as coaches and trainers for new hires?

2. What impact would the lead drivers have if used effectively as coaches or trainers?

   Follow-up question #1: What key measures or indicators would be affected?

3. What are the biggest challenges lead drivers face on the job as coaches or trainers?

4. What would you like to see emphasized in a coaching skills program for lead drivers?

FIGURE 4.6 *Interview Questions for Vice Presidents*

All items that received a rating of 3.5 or under were earmarked for training.

Phase 5: Write a Report

1. The report prepared for the HR director summarized the results of the needs assessment and provided specific recommendations for the content, skills, examples, and issues to be covered during training. The report included a proposed outline of the training program, which not only incorporated all the recommendations but also showed the sequence of topics (see Figure 4.7).

2. The report was submitted and the proposed outline approved. Some modifications were made prior to course development.

The Results

The program was well received by management and the leads because it met their identified needs. In addition, the examples used in the training came from real-life stories. The course served as a stepping stone for those leads who aspired to becoming supervisors. The company, the leads, and the drivers benefited from the program.

I. Welcome to Coaching
   A. Welcome
   B. Factors affecting how much you are able to coach
   C. Course objectives
   D. Exercise: Think about a coach you had in the past
   E. Are you coaching now?

II. The Coach as Trainer
   A. Giving directions
   B. Exercise: Benefits and drawbacks of showing and telling versus *not* showing and telling
   C. Exercise: Lessons learned

III. The Coach as Counselor
   A. Introduction
   B. The ABCs of understanding behavior
   C. Listening empathetically
   D. Giving feedback
   E. Performance coaching: A seven-step model

IV. The Coach as Motivator
   A. Leading by example
   B. Getting to know each person
   C. Incentives and rewards

V. Achieving Success
   A. Challenges faced by lead drivers in their roles as coaches
   B. Lessons learned from others
   C. When and where to coach
   D. Handling problem situations
   E. Working with your supervisor

FIGURE 4.7 *Course Outline*

CONCLUSION

A knowledge and skills assessment is one of the most basic and common forms of needs assessment conducted by HRD and HPT professionals in the workplace. This chapter has described a five-phase approach for doing such an assessment. The key to performing a successful knowledge and skills assessment is to follow a few simple guidelines.

1. *Adapt and modify your strategy based on the situation.* Although it is recommended that more than one data-gathering method be used for a needs assessment, the case in this chapter shows that a program can be successful with interviews alone.

2. *To facilitate the data-collection process, consider using existing or "found" data.*

3. *Limit the size of the group from which information must be obtained.* This simplifies the data-analysis phase considerably. If large groups must be used, be sure you have established a sound data-collection and analysis methodology.

The next chapter describes how to conduct a job and task analysis.

FIVE Job and Task Analysis

PURPOSE

This chapter will enable you to accomplish the following:

- Define a job and task analysis.

- Recognize when to use one.

- Recognize benefits and drawbacks of the approach.

- Identify critical success factors for doing a job and task analysis.

- Identify key elements, including job responsibilities and job tasks.

- Examine three phases for conducting a job and task analysis.

- Identify shortcuts to the process.

- Examine how a job and task analysis was conducted at Boehringer Mannheim Corporation.

RELATED TOOLKIT JOB AIDS

The following job aids are available in the Toolkit section of the book:

- Job Analysis Questionnaire

- Job Training and Non-Training Recommendations I (Professional/Supervisory/Management)

- Job Training and Non-Training Recommendations II (Administrative)

- Job Task Analysis Checklist

OVERVIEW

Undertaking a job and task analysis is not as difficult as it appears. After you understand what it is and how it is done, the analysis can usually be accomplished without problems.

Job analysis is a method for gathering, organizing, evaluating, and reporting work-related information (Brannick & Levine, 2002; Butruille, 1989; Fine & Cronshaw, 1999). Task analysis is a method for determining the knowledge, skills, tools, conditions, and requirements needed to perform a job (Callahan, 1985; Shepherd, 2001). Although some people consider these separate types of analyses, we combine them because of their similarities.

The primary objective of a job and task analysis is to gather information about the scope, responsibilities, and tasks for a particular job function or functions. The HRD practitioner may use this information in preparing job profiles or position descriptions. Position descriptions in turn serve as a platform for linking job requirements to current or future training needs.

Doing a job and task analysis helps people within an organization develop a clearer picture of what their jobs entail. It helps them understand what is expected of them. It also helps supervisors and managers establish criteria for job performance and thus lay a foundation for performance management and career planning systems.

The amount of time required to complete a job and task analysis can vary from a few days to several months. How much time such a project takes depends on the number of job analyses that must be developed, recognizing that each position can include many different jobs and tasks.

When to Use

A job and task analysis is most valuable under the following circumstances:

- When new or existing job descriptions or position profiles for managerial and non-managerial jobs must be developed as part of a performance management system
- When jobs must be redesigned and tasks (including the requisite knowledge, skills, attitudes, and behaviors) for each job identified
- When a consistent set of training requirements must be created, especially those involving highly technical or specialized job functions

Benefits and Drawbacks

Conducting a job and task analysis has several benefits for the organization:

- It stimulates buy-in and interest because people are directly involved in defining their jobs and tasks.
- It provides supervisors with a profile of skill sets that are necessary for people to perform competently in a given job function.
- It serves as a basis for distinguishing the skill requirements of various job classifications or levels within a position (such as entry-level versus senior positions).
- It serves as a benchmark for determining what additional knowledge, skills, attitudes, and behaviors people must acquire to move across categories or upward within a job category.

- It helps in the growth and professional development of people within an organization or a community.

The approach has drawbacks:

- It does not take into account external factors that may affect performance.
- It takes time and commitment.
- It is costly.

Critical Success Factors

A few prerequisites are crucial to the successful completion of a job and task analysis project or initiative:

- Support from senior management or senior officials
- Availability of both human and monetary resources
- A stable environment (It is difficult to question people about their jobs during downsizing, mergers, or takeovers; furthermore, their jobs and tasks may be changing.)
- Open communication about why the analysis is being prepared and how it will impact the job incumbents

Both the organization and its employees have much to gain from a job and task analysis, given the right approach and the right environment. We begin by defining a few key terms. Then we present guidelines for writing effective job task statements and standards. Finally we discuss the steps for conducting a job and task analysis.

Definition of Terms

Before we provide guidelines for writing job task statements and standards, we define a couple of terms:

- *Job responsibility.* The scope of activities for a job function or job position. For example, a job responsibility of an operations manager is to *ensure that staff members participate in the annual corporate professional education program.*
- *Job task.* What must be done to fulfill a responsibility. Usually four to six tasks are associated with each responsibility. Continuing the example of the operations manager, one job task associated with the above job responsibility is to *develop an annual professional education program for each staff member.*

WRITING JOB TASK STATEMENTS

Most people are familiar with the term *responsibilities.* For the supervisor position, one responsibility may be to manage work performance. Another may be to conduct performance reviews. Each responsibility comprises several job tasks. A job task statement essentially describes the what, why, and how of a job, as shown in the following example:

What?	Type a report
Why?	To document the minutes of a meeting
How?	By using a word-processing program

In general, it is useful to follow a few basic rules when writing job task statements:

- Restrict each sentence to one idea.
- Avoid using jargon.
- Avoid using negatives, such as "will not participate in the fund-raising campaign."

In addition, job task statements should always begin with a specific verb. Following are a few verb substitutions for increasing specificity:

INSTEAD OF	CONSIDER USING
Communicate	Write, speak
Gauge	Evaluate, identify, measure, assess, determine
Strive	Accomplish, meet, conduct

The following statements have been rewritten to begin with a specific action verb:

1. Work under direction of supervisor to develop an employee pension plan.

   Write an employee pension plan under direction of supervisor.

2. Interface monthly with business unit heads.

   Meet monthly with business unit heads.

3. Interact with treasury department to support implementation of new credit policy.

   Conduct weekly meetings with treasury department staff to support implementation of new credit policy.

4. Serve as lead for presentation of updated tariff policy plan.

   Lead presentation on the updated tariff policy plan.

WRITING STANDARDS

Occasionally, job task statements add another component—a standard—at the end of the statement. A standard specifies how a task should be performed. For instance:

- Calculate correctly the number of home closings per quarter.
- Monitor implementation of the corrective action policy by reporting employee deviations to management.
- Process new claims courteously in ten to fifteen minutes.

For example:

ASSEMBLY OF HELP DESK MANUALS

Task statement	Assemble help desk manuals.
Standards	Make twenty copies of each one-hundred-page binder using a copier, without assistance, within five business days. Insert five tab dividers into each binder in the proper places.

It is relatively easy to specify standards for administrative and technical jobs, because the degree of accuracy required for job performance is both specific and high. However, because of the time required to obtain and spell out such standards, completing a job and task analysis for a skilled worker takes longer.

KEY PHASES

There are three phases in conducting a job and task analysis:

Phase 1: Prepare

1. Identify high performers
2. Prepare job analysis questionnaire
3. Prepare materials

Phase 2: Conduct job task analysis work session

1. Prepare for the work session
2. Refine job responsibilities
3. Identify job tasks
4. Identify training and non-training requirements

Phase 3: Develop and present job training and non-training recommendations

Phase 1: Prepare

This phase consists of several tasks. Start by assembling a project team. Depending on the scope of your project, a team may be limited to you and a facilitator who leads the job and task analysis work session (see detail in Phase 2), or it can include field personnel and subject-matter experts. For high-profile projects, an advisory committee or expert panel may be necessary.

Identify High Performers

Select four to six key people in a range from above average to high performers in the job category being analyzed. The criteria for selecting high performers is explained in Chapter Six (see page 138). Occasionally, a job function expert—that is, someone within or outside the organization who is considered an expert in a particular job task—can be used as a resource. Job function experts are especially helpful when the job being analyzed is very technical or specialized.

During this preparatory stage, inform participants that they have been selected to provide input for a job and task analysis. Also inform their supervisors. If employees are located elsewhere, make travel and other arrangements. Brief participants about the process.

Prepare Job Analysis Questionnaire

Figure 5.1, Sample Toolkit Form 5.1, shows a sample job analysis survey that can be used to obtain job-related information prior to holding a work session. A week before the scheduled date of the session, distribute the survey to participants via mail, e-mail, or the Web. In addition to starting participants' thinking about the critical tasks involved in performing a job, the survey stimulates their interest in the process of job and task analysis.

TOOLKIT FORM 5.1 *Job Analysis Questionnaire*

Purpose: The purpose of this questionnaire is to gather information about your job.

Directions: Answer all the questions. Return the survey to [name/ department] by [date].

Name: _____

Sample Questions:

1. List all of your major responsibilities. Then prioritize each item by assigning a number to it. For example, assign the number "1" to the responsibility you consider the most important.

   Develop data record layouts, input forms, record formats, testing schemes, and test data.   1

   Write computer programs using logic flow charts, record layouts, and record formats.   2
   Ensure program accuracy by creating test programs, conducting spot checks, and reviewing output.   3

   Document programs, operations, and projects in accordance with company standards.   4

   Assist computer operations personnel with implementation of programs.   5

2. Why are these responsibilities important to your job?

   I need the specifications from the project lead to ensure that the logic

   programs and operating techniques I produce are efficient. I use the software

   programs and manufacturer routines in areas of sort, utility, and bulk media

   conversion. I require a PC for documentation and program development, and

   the disk storage device for creating permanent files.

3. What equipment and tools do you use in your job?

   PC computer, disk storage device, software programs, computer

   manufacturer routines, and job flow specifications from the project leader.

4. Describe some specific duties or tasks that you perform in your job, as related to your major responsibilities. List the responsibilities that you previously mentioned. After you indicate the specific duty or task, please state how often you perform this duty or task.

FIGURE 5.1 *Sample Toolkit Form 5.1: Job Analysis Questionnaire*

TOOLKIT FORM 5.1 *Job Analysis Questionnaire* (continued)

Develop data record layouts: I review and evaluate job flow specifications to make sure they are clear and that the project can be completed in the specified time. I do this about every three months.

Write computer programs: I write or modify computer programs including testing them almost daily.

Assist computer operations: I assist operations with the implementation of programs about once a week.

5. What knowledge do you require to perform your job successfully?

I need to know about accounting and manufacturing systems and data management techniques, and to have some understanding of communication concepts.

6. What qualities are necessary to make you successful in your job?

I need to be able to work in a fast-paced environment and meet deadlines.

I need to have good interpersonal skills to work with project leaders and operations personnel. I also need to be detail-oriented and to care about quality control.

7. What prior knowledge, skills, attitudes, and behaviors did you bring to your position that helped to make you successful in your job?

To be successful in this job takes either a college degree or one or more years of programming experience. You need to be aware of the latest techniques in data processing, especially if it affects programming.

8. List any courses, workshops, or training programs you attended in the past that you feel have helped you succeed in your job.

I took a communications course last year that helped me understand myself and others better. It made it easier for me to work with and understand the project leaders. I also completed a course in data management techniques, which was helpful because the field changes so frequently.

FIGURE 5.1 *Sample Toolkit Form 5.1: Job Analysis Questionnaire* (continued)

TOOLKIT FORM 5.1 *Job Analysis Questionnaire* (continued)

9. Describe any other contributing factors that you feel have made you successful in your job.

The systems project leader is very supportive. He helps me whenever I have

a question or a problem with computer operations or data conversion

personnel. He also lets me know where I stand and gives me feedback on my work.

FIGURE 5.1 *Sample Toolkit Form 5.1: Job Analysis Questionnaire* (continued)

Prepare Materials

Spend time reviewing the returned surveys and transcribe key job responsibilities from the surveys onto flip-chart paper. For example:

EMPLOYEE	PRIMARY JOB RESPONSIBILITIES
Sue	**1.** Execute marketing and strategic initiatives for asset management group.
	2. Develop advertising, direct mail, customer communication, and public relations program for asset management group products.
John	**1.** Manage product development, competitive pricing analysis, and reporting for asset management group products.
	2. Implement strategic and marketing programs worldwide for asset management group.

Phase 2: Conduct Job Task Analysis Work Session

The work session to elicit information from participants requires the use of skilled group facilitation. The primary objective of the work session is to identify key responsibilities and job tasks required for effective on-the-job performance. Once these requirements have been obtained, the group can further define the training and non-training requirements for a job.

Prepare for the Work Session

Prepare an agenda for the work session. The following sample agenda can be used as a guide. Immediately before the session, gather materials, including the prepared flip charts, completed surveys, copies of the agenda, blank flip charts, and markers. Also reserve a meeting room. When setting up the meeting room, post the prepared flip charts in a prominent place.

TIME	ACTIVITY
8:00 A.M.–8:30 A.M.	Orientation.
	• Introductions.
	• Review purpose and significance of the session.
	• Review agenda.
	• Discuss "housekeeping" issues: breaks, lunch, phone, interruptions, protocol.
8:30 A.M.–10:00 A.M.	Refine list of responsibilities.
	• Review prepared flip chart of responsibilities.
	• Brainstorm additional responsibilities.
	• Combine similar responsibilities.
10:00 A.M.–10:20 A.M.	Break.
10:20 A.M.–1:00 P.M.	Identify tasks for each job responsibility.
	• Use data from questionnaires to brainstorm tasks.
	• Review list and omit nonessential tasks.
1:00 P.M.–2:00 P.M.	Lunch break.
2:00 P.M.–3:15 P.M.	Identify the knowledge, skills, attitudes, and competencies required to perform each task.
3:15 P.M.–3:30 P.M.	Break.

3:30 P.M.–4:15 P.M.	Identify training and non-training requirements necessary to acquire the knowledge, skills, attitudes, behaviors, and competencies for each task.
4:15 P.M.–4:45 P.M.	Prioritize the training needs based on consensus about the tasks most critical to job performance.
4:45 P.M.–5:00 P.M.	Close.

- Review next steps in the process.
- Ask for subject-matter expert's availability for reviews.
- Thank participants.

Note: The time required to complete the analysis may vary. An additional half day or day may be needed, depending on the complexity of the job responsibilities, the number of participants, and the facilitator's skills.

Refine Job Responsibilities

The first order of business during a work session is to obtain consensus from participants about the key responsibilities involved in performing their jobs. The group then works to refine the list of job responsibilities posted on the prepared flip chart by combining similar statements under one statement. For example, Sue's first statement and John's second statement from the earlier example can be rewritten as follows: *Conduct marketing and strategic initiatives worldwide for the asset management group.*

Identify Job Tasks

Next, ask participants to use the information from their completed surveys to brainstorm a list of tasks for each job responsibility. Post these on a flip chart. Ask participants to review the list of tasks and delete those they consider nonessential to the job. Finally, ask participants to identify the knowledge, skills, attitudes, and behaviors required to perform each task.

Identify Training and Non-Training Requirements

Ask participants to identify the training needed to acquire the knowledge, skills, attitudes, and behaviors for each task. For example:

Position:	Project Leader
Job responsibility 1:	Manage multiple systems projects.
Job tasks:	Manage project schedules.
	Manage internal technical experts, project team, and vendors.
	Prepare interim and final reports.
Knowledge:	Project management, software architecture.
Skills and abilities:	Team leadership, resource management, oral and written communication skills.
Attitudes:	Highly motivated, future-oriented.
Behaviors:	Listen carefully to requests, record conversations in detail.
Prerequisite knowledge and skills:	Computer operating systems, client-server systems, work flow and imaging implementation.
Training required:	Advanced project management, team management, writing business reports.

Finally, ask participants to prioritize training and non-training needs on the basis of tasks they consider most critical to job performance.

Phase 3: Develop and Present Job Training and Non-Training Recommendations

The purpose of this phase is to review and organize the information obtained from the work session. Prepare a preliminary draft of the job responsibilities, the tasks, and the training and non-training recommendations. Present this draft to supervisors for review. Ask supervisors to refine the list by adding or deleting tasks. After the draft has been approved, prepare a final copy of the job training and non-training recommendations. You can use Toolkit Form 5.2 to prepare the job training and non-training recommendations for professionals and supervisory and management personnel, and Toolkit Form 5.3 to prepare the job training and non-training recommendations for administrative jobs. Figures 5.2 and 5.3 give sample job training and non-training recommendations for a marketing manager and an administrative assistant.

You may need to obtain additional approval from the human resources department. After you have received approvals from all appropriate sources, present and distribute the final statement to senior management and the target audience.

To facilitate this process, use the checklist provided in the Toolkit section, Toolkit Form 5.4, which lists the steps that should be followed when conducting a job and task analysis.

TIME-SAVING TIPS

A job and task analysis can be a time-consuming process. Following are a few ways to save time during the process:

- Ask the human resources department for a copy of any existing position descriptions, but be aware that such descriptions may or may not be current. If they are current, you can use this information to refine your survey. Asking more focused survey questions can reduce the amount of time spent in a work session.
- Eliminate one step in the process by asking participants' supervisors to attend the latter portion of a work session for the purpose of reviewing the preliminary draft of the job training and non-training recommendations statement as it is developed by the group. Doing this reduces the amount of time spent sending out the statement and waiting for approvals.

Your situation may require detailed documentation on how high-performing employees actually accomplish tasks. Such additional work analysis is often required for developing technical, systems, or managerial

TOOLKIT FORM 5.2 *Job Training and Non-Training Recommendations (Professional/Supervisory/Management)*

Job Title: Marketing Manager
Department: Marketing
Location: New York

Job Responsibility 1: Develop advertisements

1. Job Task: Define client needs

2. Job Task: Write ad copy

3. Job Task: Establish rapport with newspaper representatives

4. Job Task: Track ad response

5. Job Task: Manage advertising budget

Competencies: Grammar, understand the process of placing ads, math, organizational skills, ability to meet deadlines, interpersonal skills, word processing

Training Requirements: Features and process of writing advertisements, time management

Non-Training Requirements: Computer system for tracking

Job Responsibility 2: Develop direct mail

1. Job Task: Write promotional materials, newsletters, pamphlets

2. Job Task: Identify potential audience

3. Job Task: Maintain database

4. Job Task: Evaluate vendor services and pricing structure

5. Job Task: Track response rate

Competencies: Grammar, math, market research, database management, analytical skills, computer skills

Training Requirements: Writing, database management, marketing, desktop publishing

Non-Training Requirements: Computer tools for database management and desktop publishing

Job Responsibility 3: Maintain and develop customer communications

1. Job Task: Call customers once a quarter

2. Job Task: Respond to phone inquiries

FIGURE 5.2 *Sample Toolkit Form 5.2: Job Training and Non-Training Recommendations I*

TOOLKIT FORM 5.2 *Job Training and Non-Training Recommendations (Professional/Supervisory/Management)* (continued)

3. Job Task: Mail appropriate materials to customers

4. Job Task: Request referrals

Competencies: Interpersonal skills, ability to handle multiple tasks, follow-through skills, product knowledge

Training Requirements: Time management, communication, product information, stress management

Non-Training Requirements: Availability of needed materials

Job Responsibility 4: Develop public relations

1. Job Task: Attend Chamber of Commerce meetings

2. Job Task: Identify community charities

3. Job Task: Identify and participate in community activities

4. Job Task: Write articles for local newspapers

5. Job Task: Conduct presentations at schools, colleges, and professional meetings

Competencies: Grammar, community awareness, interpersonal skills, writing skills, assertiveness, presentation skills

Training Requirements: Assertiveness, writing, interpersonal skills, public speaking

Non-Training Requirements: Notification of Chamber of Commerce meetings, notice of deadlines for newspapers and meetings

Job Responsibility 5: Benchmark company performance

1. Job Task: Review competitors' materials

2. Job Task: Review industry literature

3. Job Task: Attend professional association meetings

Competencies: Knowledge of competition, awareness of industry publications, research techniques, analytical skills, interpersonal skills

Training Requirements: Communication, market research, interpersonal skills

Non-Training Requirements: Vendor to obtain competitors' materials, access to industry literature

FIGURE 5.2 *Sample Toolkit Form 5.2: Job Training and Non-Training and Non-Training Recommendations I* (continued)

TOOLKIT FORM 5.3 *Job Training and Non-Training Recommendations II (Administrative)*

Job Title: Administrative Assistant
Department: Accounting
Location: New York

Job Responsibility 1: Track accounts receivable

1. Job Task: Use spreadsheet to record accounts receivable

2. Job Task: Supply CFO with weekly summary report

3. Job Task: Contact delinquent accounts

4. Job Task: Reconcile ledger discrepancies

Knowledge: Accounting, math, knowledge of customer base

Skills/Abilities: Spreadsheet, word processing, interpersonal skills, organizational skills, attention to detail

Attitudes: Team player

Behaviors: Completes work and double-checking in a timely fashion

Standards: Balanced accounts, timely and accurate reports, no accounts receivable balances more than forty-five days old

Training Requirements: Accounting, math, spreadsheets, word processing, time management, procedure for contacting delinquent accounts

Non-Training Requirements: Up-to-date accounting software

Job Responsibility 2: Pay accounts payable

1. Job Task: Review invoices for accuracy

2. Job Task: Rectify invoice discrepancies

3. Job Task: Balance payable accounts

4. Job Task: Prepare and mail payments

Knowledge: Accounting, math

Skills/Abilities: Attention to detail, spreadsheet, interpersonal skills, organizational skills

Attitudes: Team player

Behaviors: Completes work and double-checking in a timely fashion

Standards: Accounts balanced, all discrepancies rectified, payments made within forty-five days of the due date

FIGURE 5.3 *Sample Toolkit Form 5.3: Job Training and Non-Training Recommendations II*

TOOLKIT FORM 5.3 *Job Training and Non-Training Recommendations II (Administrative)* (continued)

Training Requirements: Accounting, math, spreadsheets, interpersonal skills, organizational skills

Non-Training Requirements: Up-to-date accounting software

Job Responsibility 3: Prepare financial reports

1. Job Task: Review monthly records for accuracy

2. Job Task: Collect financial information for use in statistical analysis and business plans

3. Job Task: Prepare statistical summaries for management reports

4. Job Task: Duplicate and supply copies to senior management

Knowledge: Accounting

Skills/Abilities: Attention to detail, analytical skills, math, word processing, writing skills, time management, operation of the copy machine

Attitudes: Team player

Behaviors: Completes work in a timely fashion

Standards: Accurate, readable, and timely reports provided to all senior managers

Training Requirements: Accounting, company standards and practices, word processing, writing skills, time management, copy machine operations

Non-Training Requirements: Access to company standards, computer and word processing software, access to copy machine

---

Job Responsibility 4: Assist CFO with communications

1. Job Task: Prepare memos

2. Job Task: Prepare meeting summaries

3. Job Task: Monitor e-mail, internal mail, and direct inquiries

4. Job Task: Handle phone calls

Knowledge: Phone and e-mail systems, names and positions of company personnel

Skills/Abilities: Writing skills, word processing skills, organizational skills, interpersonal skills

Attitudes: Outgoing, team player

Behaviors: Completes work in timely fashion, notifies CFO of problems or delays

Standards: Memos and reports are concise, understandable, and timely; e-mail, internal mail, direct inquires, and phone calls are handled professionally

FIGURE 5.3 *Sample Toolkit Form 5.3: Job Training and Non-Training Recommendations II* (continued)

TOOLKIT FORM 5.3 *Job Training and Non-Training Recommendations II (Administrative)* (continued)

Training Requirements: Writing skills, word processing skills, phone system, e-mail, internal mail systems, organizational skills, interpersonal skills

Non-Training Requirements: Access to computer, e-mail, phone, and internal mail systems

---

Job Responsibility 5: Track sales force activity

1. Job Task: Review sales reports, compare actual sales with forecast sales

2. Job Task: Review sales expenses and compare with budget

3. Job Task: Charge expenses to appropriate customer or product accounts

4. Job Task: Prepare monthly sales expense report

5. Job Task: Calculate sales bonus and commission compensation

Knowledge: Actual sales, forecast sales, budget allowances, knowledge of customer and product accounts, compensation rates

Skills/Abilities: Analytical skills, math, word processing

Attitudes: Team player

Behaviors: Completes work in a timely fashion

Standards: Monthly sales expenses are charged to appropriate accounts; sales reports are accurate and prepared monthly; bonuses and commissions are accurately calculated by last Friday of each month

Training Requirements: Company financial reports, internal and external accounts, math, word processing

Non-Training Requirements: Timely access to company financial records, internal and external accounts

FIGURE 5.3 *Sample Toolkit Form 5.3: Job Training and Non-Training Recommendations II* (continued)

training. Examples include training operators on the exact steps of a procedure (such as how to operate a complicated machine), training employees in how to troubleshoot a process that involves many people performing interrelated tasks (such as shipping an order with many parts), or training new managers how the firm's experts perform unobservable knowledge work (such as targeting potential clients). You could document such information-intensive work by following a job and task analysis with more specific analysis procedures, such as those described by Swanson (1994).

• Stay aware of the goal for the job and task analysis and avoid collecting and analyzing data that do not relate to your goal. Notice, for example, that the case study presented shortly, which focuses only on training needs, does not analyze non-training needs.

This chapter has presented the methods and tools required to perform a job and task analysis. Take a look at how the process was actually done at Boehringer Mannheim Corporation.

CASE STUDY AND TOOLS

The information for the following case was contributed by Mary Keller, HR consultant for Boehringer Mannheim Corporation. This case shows how a job and task analysis was carried out to go beyond a set of recommendations in order to develop a training plan for a Quality Control Inspector. The end product is a position training plan.

Boehringer Mannheim Corporation (BMC) is a privately held worldwide health care device manufacturer. This biotechnology company has a diverse portfolio of "in vitro" diagnostic test systems, automated clinical chemistry systems, heterogeneous and homogenous testing, therapeutics, and biochemical products.

BMC products are used by physicians and life science research laboratories in many ways, including for diabetes monitoring, patient sample analysis, and coagulation. BMC-West, located in Pleasanton, California, researches, develops, and manufactures medical diagnostic kits. This West Coast company employs about 270 employees.

The Need

As a part of the requirements for obtaining ISO 9001 certification, the company had to meet the standard set by Element 4.19: Training.

This element, one of twenty in the standard, required employees to be qualified to perform their jobs. Documentation of their qualification was also needed.

At BMC, this requirement was satisfied by putting in place a training record system, position training plans, updated resumes, and company-wide training programs. All training systems, plans, and programs were strategically linked with the business goals of the company.

The Approach

Before examining the job and task analysis approach used by BMC to develop its position training plans, it is useful to review a couple of terms that were specific to BMC's situation.

- A *position training plan* (PTP) is a table that lists the knowledge, skills, attitudes, and behaviors needed for an individual to perform a job. It also contains the training and development activities that are necessary for acquiring minimal competencies.
- A *learning channel* is a method for acquiring knowledge, skills, attitudes, and behaviors. Learning channels are broad categories of employee and manager activities that facilitate learning and development. They include the following:

OJT	On-the-job training
A	Assignment or project
M	Mentoring or coaching
W	Workshop, class, or seminar
C	Continuing education
S	Self-directed study

To meet the requirements spelled out by a position training plan, an employee must complete the training and development activities, show evidence of previous comparable training, or demonstrate proficiency on the job. The PTPs are used as a guide by managers to identify the competencies an employee must have to perform on the job and the suggested learning channels for acquiring those competencies.

BMC took the following steps in the job and task analysis process it used to develop its position training plans.

Phase 1: Prepare

1. The human resource and quality assurance departments identified the jobs for which PTPs needed to be written. Production jobs were given priority because these jobs were more likely to be audited by the ISO review team.

2. Descriptions for the targeted jobs were completed. They included the responsibilities, the scope of decision making, and the knowledge, skills, attitudes, and behaviors for each job function.

Phase 2: Conduct Job and Task Analysis Work Session

1. Human resource consultants met with managers and supervisors in small groups to explain the function of the PTPs and how they would be developed.

2. The following process was used to develop the PTPs:

- Managers worked primarily on the PTPs for the jobs of persons reporting to them.
- Each knowledge, skill, and ability (KSA) from the job description was listed on the PTP.
- Managers then added to and refined the KSAs.

- One or more learning channels were listed next to each KSA, which permitted flexibility in planning for acquiring the new skill or knowledge and at the same time acknowledged that formal workshops or classes were not always the best way to acquire a skill.
- Comments were added (for example, a firm deadline for meeting a certain training requirement was stated).
- The human resources department reviewed the draft PTPs and issued final approvals.

Phase 3: Develop and Present Recommendations and a Job Training Plan

1. Managers and the human resources department signed the final PTPs.

2. PTPs were made available to all employees.

A sample PTP for a quality control inspector is shown in Figure 5.4.

The Results

PTPs were issued for fifty-nine nonexempt jobs in the company. The requirements for Element 4:19 of ISO 9001 were met. Job descriptions, PTPs, managers' requirements for job performance, and the training needed to develop the requisite skills for a job were firmly and logically linked.

CONCLUSION

Job and task analysis is a powerful tool that HRD and HPT practitioners can use to develop workforce potential. The information obtained from this process can serve as an important link in the evolution of many other related human development endeavors.

A job and task analysis is particularly useful in industries where jobs are highly technical or specialized. Many state and federal agencies, such as the U.S. Departments of Defense and Labor, have used the method to develop standardized training requirements for their employees.

This chapter has described a job and task analysis approach to needs assessment. It has established a context for the process by defining key terms and concepts, describing the writing of job task statements and standards, and reviewing the steps in the process. The case described a biotechnology company's experience with the analysis process and its outcomes. The next chapter presents details on undertaking a competency-based assessment.

DEPARTMENT: OPERATIONS, QA/QC

Knowledge

Training/Education	Learning Channel	Comments
High school or equivalent	C	
Basic understanding of GMPs and their application to the job	OJT, W, C, M	
Advanced working knowledge of critical and noncritical chemical inspections	OJT, A, M	Demonstrates independent judgment. Resolves problems and makes decisions and recommendations within the advanced scope of inspection.
Advanced working knowledge of packaging materials inspection	OJT, A, M	
Advanced working knowledge of packaging line, filling line, and labeling line clearance	OJT, A, M	

List what is required in each of these areas for minimal competence in performing the job:

Knowledge
- Business
- Areas of Expertise

Approved by: _____ Date: _____

HR Approval: _____ Date: _____

FIGURE 5.4 *Quality Control Inspector Position Training Plan*

SIX Competency-Based Needs Assessment

PURPOSE

This chapter will enable you to accomplish the following tasks:

- Determine the purpose of a competency-based needs assessment.

- Decide when to use the approach.

- Identify the benefits and drawbacks of the approach.

- Recognize critical success factors for performing a competency-based needs assessment.

- Explain key terms, such as *competency dictionary, core cluster, competency model,* and *individual learning development plan.*

- Identify five phases for conducting a competency-based needs assessment.

- Examine how a competency-based needs assessment was performed at Midsize Community Savings Bank.

RELATED TOOLKIT JOB AIDS

The following job aids for use with the material in this chapter are available in the Toolkit section of the book:

- Competency Project Plan Worksheet
- Competency Interview Worksheet
- Competency Dictionary Worksheet
- Competency Model Worksheet
- Individual Learning Development Plan

OVERVIEW

As a professional, you must be able to communicate and interact effectively with peers, supervisors, and internal and external customers. As a manager, you must be able to lead, solve problems, and act decisively. As a front-line supervisor, you must be able to assume ownership of customer-service problems. A competency is a knowledge, skill, attitude, or behavior that enables a person to perform effectively the activities of a given occupation or to function to the standards expected in employment (International Board of Standards for Training, Performance, and Instruction®, 2005).

Competencies and competency assessment were introduced by psychologists Robert White (1959), David McClelland (1973), and Spencer and Spencer (1993). McLagan (1980) observed, "Without clear competency criteria, recruiters select, managers manage, trainers train, and career planners plan to different (and sometimes even conflicting) images of the capabilities required to do a job" (p. 23). Today many companies, such as General Electric, Digital Equipment Corporation, the Walt Disney Company, and Hallmark Cards, have developed competency models for improving managerial and organizational performance.

The purposes of a competency-based needs assessment are as follows:

- Identify the competencies necessary for superior job performance.

- Create a composite picture or best-practice model of the competencies necessary for a particular job function or functions.

- Define incompetence and determine the knowledge, skills, attitudes, and behaviors that should be avoided for optimum performance.

In a competency-based approach, the focal point is the person, or performer. A competency-based needs assessment seeks to identify the knowledge, skills, attitudes, and behaviors the performer needs in order to excel in a job.

The time needed to complete a competency study varies. Although some studies take a few months to complete, others take several years. The amount of time needed depends on the project's scope and level of complexity.

When to Use

A competency-based approach is most effective under the following circumstances:

- *When competencies for management, supervisory, or professional jobs must be identified.* In some cases, upper management may demand that competencies be identified. In other cases, you, as the analyst, may feel that a competency approach is warranted.

- *When a credible system or "template" must be developed for recruiting, hiring, developing, and promoting individuals within specific jobs* (Boyatzis, 1982). The competency approach can aid in creating needed job specifications.

- *When the competencies for a particular professional group must be examined across many different organizations and even many different cultures and nations.* In some cases, organizations that develop training programs for specific professional groups will use a competency approach.

Benefits and Drawbacks

The benefits of a competency-based needs assessment are as follows:

- It establishes the qualities or characteristics that distinguish average from exemplary performance.
- It provides in-depth information about current and future predictors of job performance.
- It helps to increase job satisfaction because people have a clear vision of what is expected of them.
- It can be used to create standardized training and development programs.
- It can be used to develop standards and assessments for certification.

The approach has several limitations:

- It is time-consuming because it requires the involvement of many people within an organization, including managers and senior managers, and occasionally such external agencies as regulators and customers.
- It is costly to implement.
- It requires good project management skills.

Critical Success Factors

Several factors are essential to the success of a project (Griffiths, 1997):

- Competencies must produce outcomes that are consistent with the needs and goals of an organization.

- There must be a sponsor or driver who can leverage a project.

- Users must have ownership, that is, people must recognize what is in it for them.

- The model must be simple enough that people can easily access and use it.

- The model must be flexible so it can complement existing performance management systems within an organization.

Before outlining the steps for doing a competency-based needs assessment, let us review a few terms that are used in this chapter.

Competency is knowledge, skills, attitudes, or behaviors that enable one to perform the activities of a given occupation or function to the standards expected in employment. This knowledge or these skills, attitudes, or behaviors should be observable and measurable. That is, you and others should be able, for example, to test the person's knowledge, observe the person performing the skills, or determine the person's attitude through some sort of assessment.

A *performance statement* is a detailed explanation of the activities that are summarized in a competency statement (Richey, Fields, & Foxon, 2001), but it is not simply a list of tasks. For example, one of the instructional design competencies is, "Communicate effectively in visual, oral, and written form," and an associated performance statement is, "Write and edit text to produce messages that are clear, concise, and grammatically correct" (Richey, Fields, & Foxon, 2001, p. 46). In many cases, a single competency consists of certain knowledge, skills, attitudes, and behaviors. The performance statement can provide greater clarity about the specifics of the larger competency.

Domain is a cluster of related competencies grouped together under a broad dimension. For example, leadership as a domain might consist of such competencies as delegation, coaching, and team building.

A *competency model* organizes "identified competencies into a conceptual framework that enables the people in an organization to understand, talk about, and apply the competencies" (Marrelli, 1998, p. 10).

A competency model can focus on one job function (for example, sales manager), a job family (such as sales associate, sales manager, or sales executive), or multiple job families (for instance, sales, production, or research and development).

A *competency dictionary* is an organized list of definitions for individual competencies. For example, the definition of the competency *prospecting* for salespeople might read, "Evaluates current and future market conditions and uses this information to develop sales projections and goals."

An *individual learning development plan* shows the learning activities, support, resources, success indicators, and measures for improving a person's performance.

PHASES OF A COMPETENCY NEEDS ASSESSMENT

Various scholars have offered approaches for conducting a competency needs assessment. There are two main approaches:

1. Critical incident and behavioral event interviewing (Bergmann, Hurson, & Russ-Eft, 1999; Flanagan, 1954; McClelland, 1973; Russ-Eft, 2004; Spencer & Spencer, 1993)

2. Expert development and validation (Klein, Spector, Grabowski, & de la Teja, 2004; Richey, Fields, & Foxon, 2001; Rothwell, 1996)

Although both approaches focus on the knowledge, skills, attitudes, and behaviors that people must have to perform a given occupation or job function, they differ in some aspects. Readers who are interested in comparing the approaches are invited to check out the references listed above.

The following are the phases for the first approach.

Phase 1: Develop a project plan

1. Establish parameters

2. Identify key players

3. Develop work plan

Phase 2: Conduct behavioral interviews

1. Obtain preliminary information
2. Obtain behavioral information
3. Analyze behavioral information

Phase 3: Construct competency model

1. Create competency dictionary
2. Create competency model

Phase 4: Assess gaps

1. Identify gaps
2. Analyze results

Phase 5: Implement model

Phase 1: Develop a Project Plan

This phase involves refining the scope and objectives for a project, creating a project team, and establishing a project management structure.

Step 1: Establish Parameters

First, it is essential to determine the focus of the competency model and define how it will be used. This is usually done by conducting one-on-one interviews with senior management. The following questions can be asked during these interviews:

- What is the purpose of the competency study?
- How will the competency study meet the business needs of the organization?

- How many competency models must be created? For example, will a model be needed for a job function, such as sales manager; a job family, such as sales associate, sales manager, or sales executive; or multiple job families, such as sales, production, and research and development?

- For what purposes will the competency models be used? For example, will they be used for recruiting, hiring, training, performance management, or career planning?

- What resources of time, personnel, and budget are available for this effort?

- What additional constraints are anticipated, such as deadlines or input from external customers?

Step 2: Identify Key Players

After project parameters are established, identify the people who will participate in the project. Most small to medium-sized projects require a sponsor, a group of high performers, the target audience, a human resource manager, field personnel, and one or more training professionals. Large-scale projects may also require a steering committee and project liaison person to coordinate and administer a project. Subject-matter experts are required when the job content for developing a competency model is highly technical and complex terms must be translated.

High performers are the main source of information about the behaviors and actions that are necessary to do a job successfully. High performers are people who

- Consistently exceed expectations and achieve "very good" to "excellent" ratings on company performance reviews

- Consistently meet or exceed business and unit objectives

- Are informally labeled "masters" or experts by their peers and managers

- Are sought for their knowledge of or expertise in a particular subject

- Are respected by others, which is particularly important in organizations in which close teamwork is necessary

Usually human resource personnel and managers can identify high performers within an organization.

Step 3: Develop Work Plan

After key players have been identified and their availability has been determined, the next step is to develop a work plan. Figure 6.1 shows a sample high-level work plan for two hundred people. A form to scope out tasks in more detail can be found in Toolkit Form 6.1.

After the project plan is developed and approved, it is time to begin the data-collection process.

Phase 2: Conduct Behavioral Interviews

The next step involves gathering data to build a competency model. Several of the data-collection methods described in Chapter Three, such as surveys, individual interviews, focus groups, and observations, can be used.

The main advantage of surveys is that, once they are designed, they can easily be used to collect data from many different people in many different locations. However, such problems as low response rate or the lack of detailed behavioral information could diminish their effectiveness.

The main advantage of individual interviews is that detailed information can be gathered, particularly when the interviewer has the opportunity to probe and further clarify responses. However, conducting individual interviews requires a great deal of time and effort.

The main advantage of focus-group interviews is that information from many different people can be gathered at one time. However, negative group dynamics could interfere with the data-collection effort. Furthermore, focus groups may not produce a variety of views. Excellent facilitation skills and the ability to develop and ask effective questions are important prerequisites for conducting focus group interviews.

Schedule of Events - Overview (Sample)

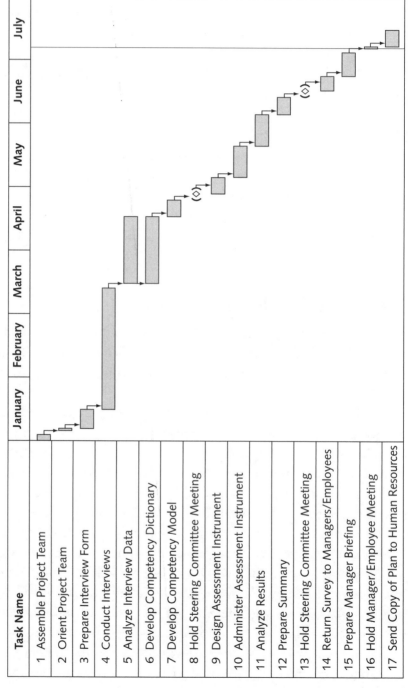

FIGURE 6.1 *Competency-Based Needs Assessment Project Plan*

The technique described in this chapter for using behavioral interviews—with individuals or groups—to gather the very specific behavioral information for building a competency model is adapted from Flanagan's (1954, 1974) Critical Incident Method. The basic purpose of behavioral interviews is to obtain two types of information from interviewees:

- Background and job-related information
- Information about what high performers do (or do not do) that makes them successful and what low performers do (or do not do) that makes them fail

There are two steps to take to obtain both types of data.

Step 1: Obtain Preliminary Information

In the beginning, it is essential to establish the right tone for an interview. Techniques for doing this include building rapport and maintaining a neutral attitude. Additional guidelines for preparing and conducting interviews are given in Chapter Three. Figure 6.2 shows a sample script you can use to start developing an actual interview. Note that the sample script is appropriate for one-on-one interviews. However, you could modify it and use it for group interviews and surveys.

After you complete this preliminary introduction, you can give participants the opportunity to talk about themselves and their job responsibilities.

Step 2: Obtain Behavioral Information

The following sample questions may be used to obtain both job-related and behavioral information. For a sample interview worksheet, see Toolkit Form 6.2 in the Toolkit section of the book.

1. What are the five main responsibilities of your job? (Probe for quantifiable results such as, "Meet sales quota every quarter.")

Thank you for agreeing to participate in this study. As mentioned in the letter you received last week, we are asking good performers to help us conduct a [name of job] competency study. The purpose of the study is to help [name of company] identify the competencies necessary for success in a [name of job] position.

We will be asking you and others what it takes to be successful in this position and what might result in failure. [Company name] would like to draw on your insights, as well as the insights of others like you, to create a best-practice model for [name of position].

This model will be used in two ways. First, we will use it to improve the hiring and selection process for [name of position]. We will use the competency criteria identified in this study to select people who are most likely to succeed in the job.

Second, we will use the model to create a training program for [name of position]. We will also develop individualized development programs to advance the skills of [name of position]. Management is committed to this very important project.

The format for collecting the information is fairly straightforward. During our interview, I will ask you to think about several critical incidents or specific situations that occurred during your work career in [name of field]. Then I will ask you to tell me two types of stories: those that led to the major successes you have experienced and those that led to unsuccessful outcomes. Please note that the information you provide will be analyzed along with that provided by other people. No individual names will be included, and no specific persons will be identified.

Before we begin, I wonder if you have any questions or concerns.

Now, before we discuss any of these incidents, I'd like to learn a little about you and your job.

FIGURE 6.2 *Sample Script for a Behavioral Interview*

Source: Adapted from *Competence at Work* by Lyle M. Spencer and Signe M. Spencer, © 1993 by John Wiley and Sons, Inc. Used by permission of John Wiley and Sons, Inc.

2. What skills and abilities do you need to accomplish each of these responsibilities? (Probe for quantifiable behaviors and actions such as, "Make five new cold calls per month.")

3. What other skills and abilities do you require to make you successful in your job? (Probe for behaviors and actions such as, "Be courteous to customers.")

4. For the next group of questions, think about a specific time [in the past week, month, or year] when you or someone else experienced success as a [position].

>   What was the context? When did it happen? Who was involved? (Probe for behaviors and actions such as, "Took the initiative, made quick decisions, listened carefully.")

>   What did you feel or think? (Probe for behaviors and actions such as, "I felt empowered and handled the problem myself.")

>   What did you say? Why were these actions and words effective? (Probe for behaviors and actions, such as, "I took the initiative and called to authorize the overdue shipment of several cartons of tape. This pleased the customer.")

>   What were the results? What significance does this event have? (Probe for behaviors and actions, such as, "I learned that by acting quickly and decisively, I saved the company from losing a customer.")

5. For the next group of questions think about a specific time [in the past week, month, or year] when you or someone else experienced failure as a [position].

>   What was the context? When did it happen? Who was involved? (Probe for behaviors and actions such as, "Failed to take the initiative, could not decide, did not listen carefully.")

>   What did you feel or think? (Probe for behaviors and actions such as, "I felt guilty, disappointed, or angry.")

>   What did you say? Why were these actions and words ineffective? (Probe for behaviors and actions, such as, "I failed to solve the customer's problem. He became angry and upset.")

>   What were the results? What significance does this event have? (Probe for behaviors and actions, such as, "I lost a good customer.")

Questions 4 and 5 can be repeated to obtain additional critical incidents.

Most interviews take between two and two-and-a-half hours to complete. Learning to develop effective follow-up questions during an interview takes time and experience. There is no comprehensive list that is appropriate for all interviews. However, here are a few suggested prompts:

- Describe for me . . .

- Tell me about a time when . . .

- Tell me about a situation that . . .

- Can you be more specific about . . . ?

- Can you give me an example of . . . ?

- What specifically happened next?

- What was your response?

- What did you think when . . . happened?

- When you said . . . , what did you mean?

- I'd like to hear more about . . .

Pitfalls to Avoid

Key to successful outcomes is avoiding the following pitfalls:

- *Using the wrong questions.* For example, asking "why" questions that require interviewees to justify, explain, or rationalize their behavior or asking leading questions.

- *Encouraging guesses.* For example, asking interviewees to guess or anticipate their future actions or reactions or asking them to guess or anticipate how others might act or react.

- *Using ineffective prompts.* For example, encouraging responses through your body language, intonations, or comments, or inaccurately paraphrasing an interviewee's responses and interrupting the interviewee with questions.

- *Making assumptions.* For example, jumping to conclusions without knowing the facts or anticipating an interviewee's next words (such as completing sentences for the interviewee).

- *Interrupting.*

Step 3: Analyze Behavioral Information

To analyze the incidents, you can follow the guidelines set forth by Flanagan (1954, 1974). These include the following:

1. Select a frame of reference. For example, later in the chapter we provide sample forms for a competency assessment on the job category "sales performance." The title serves as a frame of reference for distinguishing this competency model from one created for the job category "customer service." We recognize that in some organizations sales and customer service are aspects of the same job category. For these organizations, the frame of reference could be expanded to "sales and customer service."

2. Sort a sample of incidents into a few categories according to the selected frame of reference.

3. Develop tentative headings for major categories, for example, *leadership* and *knowledge of the industry.*

4. Sort additional incidents into these major categories and develop subcategories as needed. For example, under the leadership category you might identify *coaching* and *vision.*

5. Prepare tentative definitions for major categories, including general statements about each category. For example, the definition

for *leadership* could read, "Uses the company vision to help others achieve personal and organizational goals."

6. Decide on the level of specificity or generality to be used. For example, you could decide whether to group *listening skills* with *interpersonal* to reduce the number of major categories.

7. Redefine major categories and subcategories as needed while continuing to classify incidents.

8. After all incidents have been classified, review definitions and revise where needed.

9. Arrange to have experts in the field or a select group of interviewees complete an independent check of the classification system.

Phase 3: Construct Competency Model

The analyzed data from the previous step results in a preliminary draft of a competency model. You may want to obtain an independent check of it and enlist the client and the stakeholders in considering its applicability to the organization before you complete the two steps of this phase: create a competency dictionary and create a competency model.

Step 1: Create Competency Dictionary

Review and edit definitions that were created in the previous phase until you are satisfied with them. Finally, write an overall statement that describes each dimension. Figure 6.3 shows Toolkit Form 6.3, the Competency Dictionary Worksheet, filled out with information for a sales position. Two dimensions, *leadership* and *interpersonal,* are shown in the example. The description for the dimension *leadership* is, "Uses the company vision to help others achieve personal and organizational goals." The description for the dimension *interpersonal* is, "Projects an attitude that is positive, perceptive, and sensitive to audience needs."

TOOLKIT FORM 6.3 *Competency Dictionary—Sales*

1. Leadership: Uses the company vision to help others achieve personal and organizational goals.

Competencies/Core Clusters	Definitions
Coaching	Assists others to advance to their knowledge and skills by providing advice, encouragement, and feedback.
Influencing	Uses authority and personal charisma to gain support and commitment for goals.
Vision	Recognizes future opportunities for the organization and establishes long-term goals to maximize their potential.

2. Interpersonal: Projects an attitude that is positive, perceptive, and sensitive to audience needs.

Competencies/Core Clusters	Definitions
Articulation	Expresses facts and emotions with clarity; generates an interest in the audience.
Listening	Uses active listening skills to understand the audience's point of view and to improve communication.
Self-Awareness	Is aware of how his or her personal actions and attitudes affect others; is perceptive and understands own strengths and weaknesses.

FIGURE 6.3 *Sample Toolkit Form 6.3: Competency Dictionary Showing Two Domains for a Sales Position, Three Competencies in Each Domain, and Their Definitions*

Step 2: Create Competency Model

The model is essentially a high-level depiction of the dimensions and competencies contained in the dictionary. Note that certain positions require certain competencies while others require different competencies. Figure 6.4 shows a sample competency model for the job family *sales* using Toolkit Form 6.4. After the first draft of the competency model has been created, obtain approval from senior management and the human resources department. If necessary, make additional changes to the dictionary and the model based on their feedback. Prepare a final copy.

TOOLKIT FORM 6.4 *Competency Model—A Sales Position*

Dimensions	Competencies/Core Clusters		
	Sales Associate	Sales Manager	Sales Executive
1. Leadership Uses the company vision to help others achieve personal and organizational goals.	Influencing	Coaching Influencing	Coaching Influencing Vision
2. Interpersonal Projects an attitude that is positive, perceptive, and sensitive to audience needs.	Articulation Listening Self-awareness	Articulation Listening Self-awareness	Articulation Listening Self-awareness

3. Knowledge of the Industry
Maintains an up-to-date understanding of the industry by reading industry journals, attending meetings and conventions, and networking.
	Product and
	  service
	  knowledge
	Market
	  knowledge
		Product and
		  service
		  knowledge
		Market
		  knowledge
			Product and
			  service
			  knowledge
			Market
			  knowledge

4. Management Uses company resources and personnel to meet or exceed company goals.	Decision making	Decision making Budget control Staffing Team building	Decision making Budget control Staffing Team building
5. Sales Skills Meets or exceeds sales goals by anticipating and responding to clients' needs for services and products.	Prospecting Presentation Persuasion Customer service	Presentation Persuasion Customer service	Presentation Persuasion Customer service
6. Personal Attributes Possesses values, attitudes, qualities, and behavior that are consistent with the industry and the organization's standards.	Initiative Integrity Flexibility	Initiative Integrity Flexibility	Initiative Integrity Flexibility

FIGURE 6.4 *Sample Toolkit Form 6.4: Competency Model for a Sales Position*

Phase 4: Assess Gaps

When the competency model is complete, you can use it to identify the gaps in the proficiencies of individuals who perform the job functions. It is only after these gaps have been identified that appropriate interventions can be developed to close them. This phase consists of two steps: identify gaps and analyze results.

Step 1: Identify Gaps

As explained in Chapter One, a gap is the difference between an actual condition and an ideal condition, or the difference between what performance is and what performance should be. Surveys are an effective tool for gathering this type of data. You will need to decide who should receive the survey. You may want to involve all of the key players mentioned earlier or you may want to involve the target group only.

Figure 6.5 shows a simple rating scale that can be used to obtain information. Note that in an actual survey the competencies that were identified in the competency assessment would be listed in the left column.

Note that the survey could use other types of scales, such as "How important is this competency for success on the job?" or "How frequently do you do this competency?" or both.

Step 2: Analyze Results

After the surveys have been distributed and returned, data can be analyzed by using one of the software packages that are available for this purpose, or they can be tabulated by hand. As discussed in Chapter Three, you may want to examine the frequency of responses, a measure of central tendency (such as the average, median, or mode), and a measure of variability (such as the standard deviation, the quartile range, or the range). If you surveyed people from different groups (such as the top performers and the average performers in the job), you may want to examine the differences among the groups.

SAMPLE SURVEY QUESTIONS

Instructions: On the following rating scale, fill in the bubble that corresponds most closely to the degree with which you agree or disagree that the statement represents a critical part of the job.

	Strongly Disagree	Disagree	Neutral	Agree	Strongly Agree	Not Applicable
Coaching: Assists others in advancing their knowledge and skills by providing advice, encouragement, and feedback.	◯	◯	◯	◯	◯	◯
Influencing: Uses authority and personal charisma to gain support and commitment to goals.	◯	◯	◯	◯	◯	◯

FIGURE 6.5 *Sample Rating Scale*

> **Tip**
>
> Reviewing an actual competency assessment could provide useful insights for your project. Russ-Eft (2004) described a competency assessment that involved 460 customer service providers from companies in North America, Europe, and Asia.

Phase 5: Implement Model

Competency models have many applications. They can be used to create individual development plans and to develop selection, hiring, and other performance-management systems. Here we discuss one application: individualized learning development plans.

The first step in developing individualized learning development plans is to share the employees' completed surveys with managers. After managers receive a copy of the survey results, a brief meeting can be held with them to explain how to develop and use learning development plans. During this meeting, copies of the Toolkit Form 6.5, Individual Learning Development Plan, can also be distributed. Managers can adapt the following agenda to conduct a meeting with employees:

1. Review individual areas of strengths and identify opportunities for development.

2. Identify the support and resources required to facilitate performance.

3. Develop an action plan that best meets the needs of the learners.

4. Create a schedule for implementing learning and development activities.

5. Discuss a follow-up plan.

After a competency model has been implemented, results can be monitored at both the organizational and individual levels. At the individual level, managers can conduct quarterly or annual progress checks with their employees. At the organizational level, the impact of the assessment can be measured using other data, such as client satisfaction surveys or reorders or whatever might be relevant to the employees.

The preceding sections presented the methods and tools for conducting a competency-based assessment. Now it is time to see how it was actually done at Midsize Community Savings Bank.

The information for this case was contributed by Anne Marie Dyckman, director of human resources at Midsize Community Savings Bank. Although most of the case events are real, the name of the bank is fictitious. The goal of the case study was to develop a competency model for branch managers. The key tools shown here are the competency dictionary and the competency model. The case study shows that the competency-based approach to needs assessment can be implemented flexibly. For example, the manager's skills in this case were assessed after the competency model was implemented.

Midsize Community Savings Bank is a Federal Deposit Insurance Commission (FDIC) state-chartered bank with more than $1 billion in assets. Historically a mortgage bank, it later changed to commercial lending activities. The bank has eighteen branch locations, each headed by a branch manager. Only sixteen branch managers participated in the competency study.

The Need

The president of the bank recognized that branch managers required a core set of competencies in order to be effective. He also recognized that managers possessed these competencies, but to differing degrees. Further, the bank president wanted to establish a standardized method for selecting new candidates for the branch manager position.

A competency needs assessment was expected to provide a model of best practices for branch managers. The model would also serve as a resource for creating a training curriculum and as an aid for senior management in making better choices when hiring new candidates.

The Approach

The project-planning and competency-modeling processes for Midsize Community Savings Bank were divided into four phases:

Phase 1: Develop a project plan
Phase 2: Conduct behavioral interviews
Phase 3: Construct the competency model
Phase 4: Implement the model

Phase 1: Develop a Project Plan

1. The HR director met with the bank president and senior managers to determine how the project fit with the business goals and strategies. It was decided that the HR director would work with management to determine business issues and relevant measures.

2. The HR director developed a project plan that included the size, scope, responsibilities, and time that would be needed to complete the project.

Phase 2: Conduct Behavioral Interviews

1. The president of the bank and the HR director identified the best possible sources of interview data. They also identified the best candidates for the competency study.

2. The HR director interviewed selected individuals and asked them to provide examples from their past that showed a specific time when a skill or behavior was used. The director obtained a detailed list of the critical knowledge, skills, attitudes, and behaviors that allowed branch managers to succeed.

Phase 3: Construct the Competency Model

The HR director completed the following steps:

1. Organized and ordered the interview data by identifying similarities and patterns in behavioral data
2. Prepared a draft of the completed template
3. Edited the content and grouped common themes
4. Created competency definitions and developed a competency dictionary (as shown later in the chapter)
5. Created the first draft of the competency model
6. Presented the first draft of the dictionary and model to senior management
7. Made appropriate revisions
8. Presented the final dictionary and competency model to senior management (see Figure 6.6 for the branch-manager competency model)

Primary and secondary competencies for branch managers were identified. Primary competencies were considered essential to success on the job. They included self-confidence, initiative, achievement orientation, conceptual thinking, creative thinking, sound business understanding, customer-service orientation, and interpersonal understanding. Secondary competencies were considered important to the job. They included information seeking, leadership, teamwork, and cooperation.

Implement Model

A profile of a successful branch manager was developed. This profile served as the basis for a new selection process. Using a five-item rating scale ranging from "very strong evidence skill is not present" to "very strong evidence skill is present," potential candidates could be assessed on their ability to perform effectively in a branch manager position.

The competency model also served as the basis for a performance appraisal system that used a seven-item Likert-type scale ranging from 1 = fails to 7 = exceeds. In addition, the model was used to establish a framework for training.

Dimensions	Competencies			
1. Personal	Self-confidence	Initiative	Achievement orientation	
2. Thinking	Conceptual thinking	Information seeking	Creative thinking	
3. Technical	Sound business understanding			
4. Relational	Customer service orientation	Leadership	Interpersonal understanding	Teamwork and cooperation

FIGURE 6.6 *Competency Model: Branch Manager*

CONCLUSION

Organizations must have ways to maximize human capital by identifying and closing gaps in performance. Performance gaps can be measured more easily when an ideal model exists.

The competency-based approach helps an organization define the knowledge, skills, attitudes, and behaviors necessary for people to perform efficiently in their jobs. The results can be applied in many ways to achieve higher levels of performance. This chapter has shown how individual learning development plans can be created after a competency model has been built. The case study described how a competency-based needs assessment was used to improve candidate selection, the performance appraisal system, and training for new and existing managers in a bank.

The chapter described a process for identifying the competencies necessary for people to perform successfully in their jobs. The focus was on the ways an individual performed in his or job. In the next chapter, on strategic needs assessment, the focus changes to examining the larger organization as well as the individuals within that organization.

SEVEN Strategic Needs Assessment

PURPOSE

This chapter will enable you to do the following:

- Describe the purpose of a strategic needs assessment.

- Recognize when to use the approach.

- Identify the benefits and drawbacks of the approach.

- Recognize critical success factors for performing a strategic needs assessment.

- Identify five phases for conducting a strategic needs assessment.

- Examine how a strategic needs assessment was performed at the fictitious Company XYZ.

RELATED TOOLKIT JOB AIDS

The following job aids for use with the material in this chapter are available in the Toolkit section of the book:

- Business Issues Worksheet
- Fisher's Models of Organizational Performance Worksheet
- Process Map Worksheet
- Gap Analysis Worksheet
- Change Readiness Checklist
- Performance Improvement Planner

OVERVIEW

Organizational leaders use strategic thinking and planning to anticipate issues and situations so they can shape them and gain competitive advantage. Every organization faces a variety of performance problems during the course of its business cycle. The scope and magnitude of these performance problems differ, but when the problems affect core business processes, using quick-fix solutions to close performance gaps can be harmful. In such situations, strategic interventions are necessary.

Before implementing a strategic intervention to improve performance, it is essential to examine performance gaps within the context of the marketplace and the total business operation. Only then can appropriate solutions be prescribed and a road map for closing the gaps be followed.

A strategic needs assessment examines the internal and external factors that affect performance within the context of an organization's business strategy and identifies the gaps between the current and desired conditions. Closing these gaps is critical for an organization's long-term success.

While many people view strategic needs assessment as a systematic approach for determining the strategic or operational needs of a business firm, it can also be used in other types of organizations, such as an organizational unit, a nonprofit organization, a country, a community, or an interorganizational entity.

Implementing a strategic needs assessment requires partnership between the analyst who implements the needs assessment and the client who is responsible for business results. What does the analyst bring to the partnership? Credibility, trust, HRD and HPT knowledge and skills, and a deep knowledge of the business (Robinson & Robinson, 2006).

When to Use

A strategic needs assessment is most effective in the following situations:

- When performance improvement needs are linked to the business strategy of an organization
- When the organization is undertaking long-term performance improvement or organizational change initiatives
- When processes that do not add value to an organization must be identified

Benefits and Drawbacks

Doing a strategic needs assessment offers many benefits. For example, it allows an organization to do the following:

- Develop long-term solutions to existing performance problems or new performance needs.
- Solve problems that affect core business processes, such as product development, order processing, or service delivery.

The main drawbacks to the approach are as follows:

- It can be time-intensive.
- It often requires participation by many people.
- It might be costly.

- It requires the analyst to use advanced organization development skills.

Critical Success Factors

The success of a strategically focused project depends on several factors:

- Sponsorship from executive management
- Proactive participation of senior and line managers
- Access to resources such as customers, suppliers, and business resources
- Organizational readiness to change

Following are a few terms that will be used in the chapter:

- *Mission:* A broad statement describing an organization's future plans and directions
- *Business goal:* A statement describing a measure or target that will be achieved during a certain period, for example: "$100 billion in revenue by the year 2010"
- *Business unit:* A department or function within an organization, such as production or operations
- *Business process:* A series of activities that provide products, deliver services, or manage resources, such as handling accounts receivable within the finance business unit
- *Process map:* A graphic illustration of the steps or activities that are performed in a business process (see the example in Figure 7.6 later in this chapter)
- *Process boundary:* An arbitrary "line" that shows where a business process begins and where it ends, such as the process boundary for an order management process that begins when the customer-service unit sends a mail order and ends when a product is received by a customer

- *Performance improvement planner:* A blueprint that documents all the performance-improvement projects that must be undertaken to improve the overall effectiveness of an organization

KEY PHASES

A strategic needs assessment has five phases:

Phase 1: Gather preliminary information about the situation

Phase 2: Examine external environment

Phase 3: Examine internal environment

1. Validate business strategy
2. Document current performance
3. Identify causes of performance gaps

Phase 4: Chart future environment

Phase 5: Develop performance improvement plan

1. Assess readiness for change
2. Select interventions

In the workplace, some organizations have comprehensive and useful strategic plans and other organizations have not yet completed their plans. Because a strategic needs assessment relies on a thorough understanding of the organization's strategy, the following discussion of the phases and the steps within them includes background information on strategic planning.

Phase 1: Gather Preliminary Information About the Situation

The purpose of this phase is to develop a better understanding of a current or future performance need. For example, a 30 percent increase in customer complaints would indicate that a current problem exists. A mandate from senior management stating that a company's workforce must be prepared for the demographic changes that will occur by 2012 would indicate a future performance need.

During this phase, it is not necessary to seek information from too many people. Discussions with a few key people will provide enough data to establish preliminary process boundaries and a definition of the performance problem or opportunity. A good first action is to conduct interviews with a few senior executives from the involved business unit. Later, the span of inquiry can be widened to include middle management and first-line supervisors. Toolkit Form 7.1 contains an interview worksheet, The Business Issues Worksheet, that could be used to examine an existing performance problem or to address a future performance need. Figure 7.1 offers five questions from that worksheet.

You can also obtain supporting information from secondary sources, such as transcripts of conversations with customers. After you complete a preliminary analysis, it is important to document your findings in a report that includes the following elements:

- The background of the problem or need
- The scope of the problem or need
- The performance improvement goals
- The evidence examined

TOOLKIT FORM 7.1 *Business Issues Worksheet*

- What are the key business issues that must be addressed?
- What are the consequences of not taking action?
- Which business processes are currently affected?
- What are the performance improvement goals?
- What prevents the achievement of business goals?

FIGURE 7.1 *Toolkit Form 7.1: Business Issues Worksheet—Sample Questions*

Use the information in the report to plan the remaining phases of the needs assessment.

Phase 2: Examine External Environment

Many external factors can affect organizational performance. During Phase 2, information is collected on external factors, and these data are analyzed. The purpose of this phase is to

- Identify and isolate external factors affecting a performance need.
- Determine the implications of these external factors.

Porter's classic (1980) Five Forces model offers a useful framework for performing this type of analysis in organizations. According to Porter's model, organizations are affected by five forces:

- New competitors who could erode an organization's profitability or market share
- Major suppliers or supply chains that could raise costs or control the availability of products
- Substitute products or services that could cause demand for a product to fall
- Customers who could switch to other products, thus causing profits to drop
- Competition among industry players

Note that organizational units can also face these forces. A full-fledged five forces analysis is beyond the scope of this book but, as Figure 7.2 shows, the model serves as a useful framework for determining the threats and opportunities that could impede or enhance organizational performance. It also helps to identify the critical business issues that must be considered when developing a solution to a performance opportunity or need.

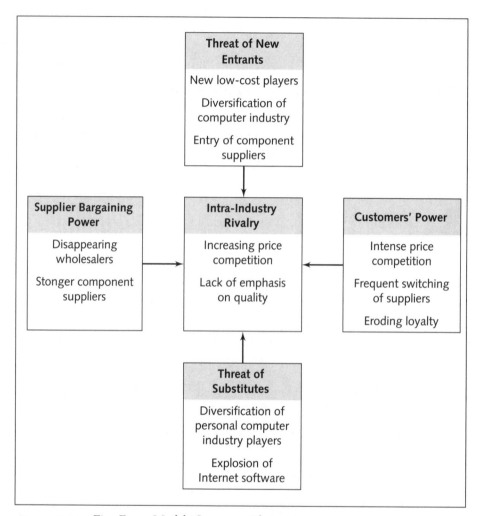

FIGURE 7.2 *Five Forces Model: Consumer Electronics*

Source: Adapted with permission of The Free Press, a Division of Simon & Schuster, from
Competitive Strategy: Techniques for Analyzing Industries and Competitors, by Michael E. Porter.
Copyright © 1980 by The Free Press.

For example, potential threats to a company in the consumer electronics industry include new and potential entrants (such as the emergence of new technologies), diversification of the computer industry, and entry of new suppliers (refer to the top box of Figure 7.2). Similarly, price wars, as shown in the box titled "Customers' Power," can result in loss of customers.

Usually, information pertaining to the external forces (that is, the five forces) affecting a performance problem or need can be obtained from discussions with the senior leaders of a company. The following existing sources can also be used:

- Industry reports

- Industry conferences and proceedings

- Business newspapers, such as the *Wall Street Journal*

- Dow Jones Industrial Index

- Specialized trade journals

- Market research data

- Customer-satisfaction surveys

- Notes from meetings with customers or suppliers

- In-house sales or purchasing databases

- Secret shoppers

- Dun and Bradstreet reports

- SEC reports

When using the Five Forces model, it is also helpful to remember that other forces, such as governmental and regulatory restrictions, can affect a performance need. For instance, a new regulatory bill can cause a slowdown in customer purchases that in turn can result in lower profits. As Porter (1980) suggested, these additional factors should be examined within the context of the five main factors listed earlier.

Phase 3: Examine Internal Environment

Phase 3 provides answers to the questions *What is the organization's competitive strategy given its external environment? Which business processes are affected by the performance problem or performance need?* and *What are the performance gaps?* Depending on the scope of the performance need, this phase can take a few days or several months to complete. It has three steps: validate the business strategy, document current performance, and identify causes of performance gaps.

Step 1: Validate Business Strategy

Business strategies are the sets of policies, plans, and directions that the organization uses to achieve its business goals. They can be found in the business plan. Figure 7.3 shows an outline for a simple business plan.

The organization's business strategy sets the direction for learning and performance-improvement initiatives. Organizational goals and goals across levels, units, and processes should be aligned (Gephart & Van Buren, 1996; Rummler & Brache, 1995). Problems often arise when there is misalignment.

Business plans can be very detailed. For examples, see the business plans at the U.S. Small Business Administration Web site, http://sba.gov. When reviewing a business plan, focus your attention on the strategies and tactics that pertain to your particular project. For example, if you are seeking to discover reasons for declining production, examine the section of the business plan that contains production goals. If a business plan is not available or if the information is dated, you could conduct individual or group interviews with senior executives to obtain these data.

Step 2: Document Current Performance

This step in a strategic needs assessment focuses on documenting, or mapping, exactly how current performance occurs. The process of documenting the elements and relationships that affect your organization's particular need can make obvious the deficiencies and discrepancies in the performance system.

Mission

Become the most powerful and service-oriented retail company.

Become the leader in every global market served by the end of the decade.

Business Goal

Gain 10 percent of market share by the end of the fiscal year and 20 percent of market share by the end of the second fiscal year.

Introduce three new lines of consumer products by the end of this fiscal year.

Reduce the cost of manufacturing our top three products by 30 percent.

Other components of a business plan:

- Critical success factors

- Market analysis

- Competitive analysis

- Tactical analysis

- Financial analysis including cash flow (actual and projected)

- Head count plan

- Profit and loss statement (actual and projected)

- Balance sheet (actual and projected)

FIGURE 7.3 *Outline of a Simple Business Plan*

Figure 7.4 shows sample performance measures that can be used to document business process activities during this stage of the analysis. As the figure illustrates, the quality of services provided by an accounting unit can be measured by the number of errors per bill. In the same way, customer satisfaction can be measured by the number of invoices that were incorrect. Any deviation from a stated objective is an indication that a problem exists.

An organization is composed of hundreds of processes; therefore, mapping performance is no simple undertaking. However, as Mankins and Steele (2005) point out, performance bottlenecks are often invisible to top management. Moreover, without good information about how

Process	Cost	Quality	Customer Time	Satisfaction
Accounting/Billing	Bills processed per person	Number of errors processed per bill	Amount of time taken to process a bill	Number of bills generated incorrectly
Treasury/Accounts Receivable	Bank reconciliation per person	Percentage of receivables outstanding past ninety days	Average number of days sales outstanding	Number of posting errors
Production	Average cost per unit below ten cents	Number of defects produced per billion	Amount of orders shipped on time	Number of returns per thousand units sold

FIGURE 7.4 *Sample Performance Measures*

and why poor performance is occurring, top management finds it virtually impossible to implement appropriate corrective action.

In a hierarchical organization, some processes cross individual, group, and organizational levels. Examples include activities that contribute to high-level organization processes (such as product launches that typically involve marketing, product development, and sales), groups that contribute to the overall organization (such as human resources), and individuals who contribute to group processes. Some processes occur at the same level but involve different aspects of performance, such as a team accomplishment that also increases its learning and its capacity for future accomplishment.

Many tools are available for documenting current performance. Four that provide especially powerful insights are (1) Organizational Performance Models, (2) the SIPOC diagram, and (3) process mapping.

Organizational Performance Models. Fisher's (2000) theory of organizational performance in for-profit organizations contains models that are useful for mapping current performance at the individual, group, and organizational levels. At each level, these models show the aspects of performance that reflect our current understanding of systems theory (that is, capacity, production process, learning process, and accomplishments). Fisher's models also show cross-level performance relationships.

Toolkit Form 7.2 contains the Fisher models (Fisher, 2000; Fisher & Sleezer, 2003) and provides a brief description of each. Use these models to map the processes for your particular situation, to show how your performance need is linked to organizational performance, and to point out where potential deficiencies and discrepancies in a performance system might be occurring. In addition to providing visual images, the models contain useful language for discussing the processes that contribute to a particular performance need.

When using these models, pay attention to how learning and performance changes are transferred. For example, a needs assessment that recommends improving an organization's performance by training individuals should specify the processes by which such learning improves organizational performance. It should detail exactly how increased individual knowledge and skills will produce increased individual performance and also exactly how increased individual performance will eventually increase organizational performance.

Measurement is important when specifying how learning and performance improvements transfer to performance. For example, are individual behaviors pooled to achieve organizational performance? Or are they averaged? Or does performance emerge from a complex combination of diverse individual contributions into team performance that is subsequently transferred to organizational performance? The answers depend on the situation.

Mapping precisely how the transfer of learning and improved performance actually occurs in a complex organization requires some heavy-duty analysis work. However, this work is important because breakdowns in the transfer-of-learning and the transfer-of-performance processes result in wasted resources.

> **Tip**
>
> When mapping organizational performance, save time by starting with the accomplishments that are delivered to the product market.

SIPOC Diagram. *SIPOC* stands for *s*uppliers, *i*nputs, *p*rocess, *o*utputs, and *c*ustomers. This tool reflects the systems view of organizations that was discussed in Chapter One and is useful for finding out and documenting at a high level the inputs, outputs, and work flows of a specific process. Start by asking about the outputs:

- What results or outputs does the process deliver?
- What inputs are required to make the process successful?
- Who provides the inputs to the process?
- Who are the customers of the process?
- What do the customers of this process require?
- What steps are involved in completing the process?

A SIPOC Map for car repair created by the U.S. Army Operation Oversight Office is shown in Figure 7.5.

The steps for completing a SIPOC process flow are as follows:

1. Use the information gathered during Phases 1 and 2 of the strategic needs assessment to define the scope of the project and the specific process you will examine.

2. Use the *outputs* to define the end point of the process and the *inputs* to define the starting point for the process. The SIPOC will

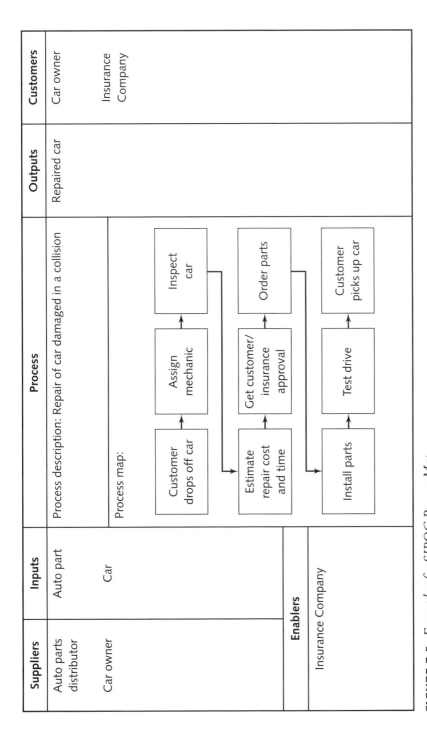

Suppliers	Inputs	Process	Outputs	Customers
Auto parts distributor	Auto part	Process description: Repair of car damaged in a collision	Repaired car	Car owner
Car owner	Car	Process map:		Insurance Company

Customer drops off car → Assign mechanic → Inspect car

Estimate repair cost and time → Get customer/ insurance approval → Order parts

Install parts → Test drive → Customer picks up car

Enablers

Insurance Company

FIGURE 7.5 *Example of a SIPOC Process Map*

Source: http://www.army.mil/aeioo/cpi/tools.htm#three

not identify processes that occur before the starting point or after the end point.

3. Record the process *outputs,* or results, and the *customers* who receive them.

4. Record the process *inputs* and the *suppliers* for each input.

5. Record the supports, or *enablers,* for the process.

6. Label the SIPOC process flow with a title identifying the process it illustrates.

7. Review the completed SIPOC process flow with the project sponsor and other involved stakeholders for verification.

Process Mapping. One major reason for performance gaps is activities that do not contribute to business or customer needs. Non-value-added activities result in waste and increased costs. These activities must be understood and documented so that gaps in performance can be minimized. Simple real-life examples of non-value-added activities include unnecessary duplication of tasks; idle or waiting time when no task is being performed; and checking, logging, or approving tasks that were performed correctly.

A process map uses graphic symbols, such as ovals and arrows, to show the steps of a process and the flow of information. A process boundary shows where a process begins and ends. For example, the process boundary for order management in an organization begins when a customer-service unit sends a mail order and ends when the product is received by a customer. You can use Toolkit 7.3 as an aid in mapping a process. As an example, the process for filling a customer's order in one organization is shown in Figure 7.6.

Tip

Many software packages are available that quickly and easily produce process maps (for example, Visio and Corel Flow).

TOOLKIT FORM 7.3 *Process Map Worksheet*

A process map uses graphic symbols to show the steps of a process. It also shows where a process begins and ends. Following are the graphic symbols to use:

1. To show information received from a source OUTSIDE a process boundary, such as a customer, customer request, or another business unit, use a RECTANGLE.

2. To show any activity that is being carried out WITHIN a process, such as completing a form, use an OVAL.

3. To show the FLOW between activities (INPUTS and OUTPUTS), use an ARROW.

TIPS FOR PROCESS MAPPING

1. Before mapping a process, define the starting and ending points and the level of detail that is needed.

2. Document steps in sequence. Try to restrict your diagram to major steps at first. Do not become bogged down in too much detail.

3. Begin by identifying the output and the input. Then identify the first major process activity, such as processing quotes, as shown in Figure 7.6. Determine the flow of information to and from this process. Use single-pointed arrows for information that flows in one direction. For information that flows between two units or processes, use two-pointed arrows.

4. Identify the next major process. Document the inputs and outputs to this process.

5. Link all major processes as well as inputs and outputs.

6. If you cannot define intermediate steps, make notes. Come back to this step later.

7. When you have finished creating your process map, retrace steps to verify accuracy of information collected.

8. Review the process map with the project sponsor and other involved stakeholders for verification.

FIGURE 7.6 *Sample Toolkit Form 7.3: Process Map Worksheet for an Order Management Process*

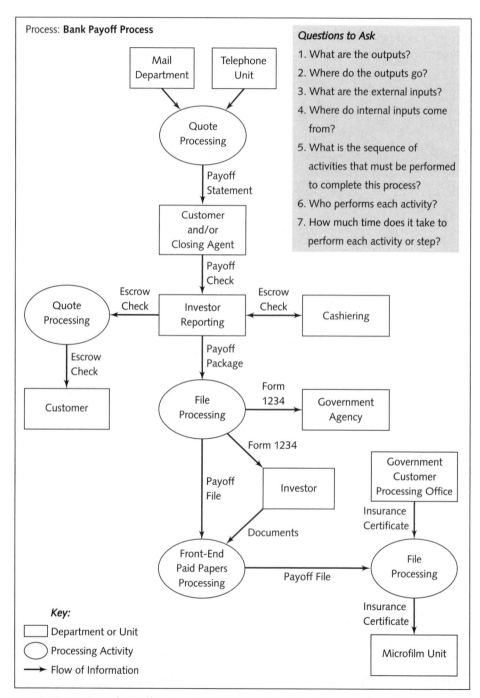

FIGURE 7.6 *Sample Toolkit Form 7.3: Process Map Worksheet for an Order Management Process* (continued)

When completing a process map, it is important to maintain perspective about how much detail is needed. You need to capture all the details that matter but avoid wasting time in documenting extra details that do not provide relevant information for your problem or need.

Once a process map is completed, it should be examined to identify such opportunities for performance improvement as bottlenecks, weak links, poorly defined activities, and activities that do not add value. Also, the map can be used to document responsibilities, standards, and measures for each step of the process.

> **Tip**
>
> If you plan to institute a new process or improve a process in an organization, consider benchmarking industry leaders. Benchmarking is a process of measuring the products and processes of industry leaders using specified standards and using the information to improve your product or process. When benchmarking, be sure to consider the larger systems because a product or process that works well for one organization may not do well in another organizational system.

Step 3: Identify Causes of Performance Gaps

Comparing the current documented performance to the ideal, future, or expected performance reveals the existence, location, and nature of gaps in such areas as quality of equipment, completeness of available information, and worker knowledge, skills, attitudes, and behaviors. Techniques such as root cause analysis, brainstorming, and a Fishbone diagram and procedure analysis can be useful in uncovering the real cause of problems and thus produce significant long-term performance improvement.

Root cause analysis was developed from the insight that most often symptoms of performance problems rather than their underlying causes are addressed. Root cause analysis is a procedure for identifying the most probable causes of problems so organizations can eliminate them rather than continue to deal with their symptoms. The procedure involves continuing to ask "Why?" until the pattern becomes evident and the causes of the problem become obvious.

Brainstorming is a method of problem solving in which group members contribute ideas spontaneously. To encourage creativity, the ideas are not evaluated or discussed until everyone has contributed. Often an idea that originally seemed far-fetched leads to the solution.

A *Fishbone, or Ishikawa, diagram* is used to show all the causes (or inputs) for a single problem. Figure 7.7 shows a sample fishbone diagram. To create such a diagram, first fill in the problem statement, which in this example is that workers are dissatisfied. Then identify all the categories of problems, which in the example are management, manpower, materials, and machines. Then show causes of the problem and arrange them by category and by their level of importance. The result is a picture that shows relationships among the potential causes of a problem.

Procedure Analysis. Procedure analysis is a systematic process for documenting step-by-step the process for completing a complex or important task. Often the subject expert demonstrates the task and the analyst records the steps that are performed to complete the task. Swanson (1996) provides information on how to conduct such an analysis.

To document Phase 3 activities, use Toolkit Form 7.4. (See Figure 7.8 for a sample of the form.)

When a pump manufacturing firm found a higher number of defects in its popular small pump, the division vice president told the chief learning officer (CLO) to "Fix it, *now!*" As a first step, the CLO conducted a speedy strategic needs assessment. He examined the external environment by talking with the vice president of marketing and reviewing some industry reports. He learned that the demand for the pumps had increased and would likely remain strong. Product defects were the major problem in retaining customers. Looking internally, the CLO found that

- Many new workers had been hired and more new hires were expected.
- Training new hires was done on the job using knowledgeable workers who had previously been trained by the product engineer or the director of quality.
- The parts acquisition process had not changed.

To document current performance, the CLO asked the director of quality and the product engineer to demonstrate the procedure for assembling the pump. At first they did not see the need for the demonstration, but they eventually agreed to do it and gathered the parts for assembling two pumps.

Interestingly, just before beginning the demonstration, the director of quality joked with the product engineer that performance would really improve when all employees could assemble pumps as well as they did. You can almost guess what happened next. While demonstrating the correct assembly steps, these subject experts saw that they each used different procedures. They first hotly argued about whose procedure caused more defects. They then decided to work together to improve the assembly process, which the CLO documented using procedure analysis. The resulting document was used to train employees, which, in turn, resulted in fewer defective pumps.

Phase 4: Chart Future Environment

After deficiencies and causes of performance gaps have been identified, start documenting the desired processes and performance. The map created in this phase is a reconfigured process map at the same level of detail as the one created in the previous phase. Usually, new organizational

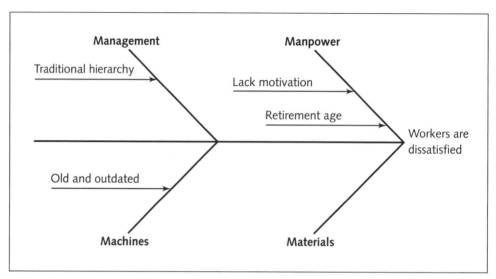

FIGURE 7.7 *Sample Fishbone Diagram*

charts, job classifications, performance measures, or team structures are needed to support a new system. Minimizing unnecessary specialization and rigidity in job content can improve performance at the organizational, process, and job levels. To access guidelines for performing an analysis at the job and task levels, see Chapter Five.

Phase 5: Develop Performance-Improvement Plan

In this phase the analyst essentially transforms the information that was mapped in the earlier phase into a performance improvement plan, a blueprint, that documents all the performance-improvement projects that must be undertaken to improve the overall effectiveness of an organization. This phase involves two steps: assess readiness for change and select interventions.

Step 1: Assess Readiness for Change

First, it is essential to assess whether an organization and its people are ready to implement a performance improvement plan. A formal plan to determine change readiness is particularly necessary when the performance-improvement plan will require significant changes in pro-

TOOLKIT FORM 7.4 *Gap Analysis Worksheet*

Process	Current Performance Indicators	Performance Gap	Effect
Quote processing	5 business days	Customers expect quote within 2 days	Lost business; dissatisfied customer
Escrow check processing	7 business days	Tax data not received on time	Processing delay
File processing	10 business days	Payoff package incomplete	Processing delay

FIGURE 7.8 *Sample Toolkit Form 7.4: Gap Analysis Worksheet*

cesses, systems, or jobs. For example, the implementation of a new call-management system may involve establishing standards and instituting a training program, a communications program, and a performance-management system.

Making obvious preparations for change is a strategy for building trust among people who will be affected by the change. Creating or maintaining an open work climate will help to minimize people's resistance to change. When launching a change initiative, it is usually best to assign the initiative to a project leader or facilitator who can manage the whole effort. See Toolkit Form 7.5 for a checklist that can be used to guide this effort.

Step 2: Select Interventions

Next, it is necessary to select the interventions that will most effectively support the implementation of a performance-improvement plan. The performance-improvement planner is a useful tool when undertaking this task. Toolkit Form 7.6 shows the factors that must be considered, such as critical success factors, prerequisites for starting a project, and other related project requirements. Using this systematic approach allows the value and cost of each performance-improvement project to be assessed quickly and easily.

This chapter has presented the methods and tools for doing a strategic needs assessment. Here is how it was done at XYZ Corporation.

This fictitious case was contributed by Bob Carroll, an organizational consultant. Carroll has been involved in several performance improvement initiatives for a major computer company. The key tools shown here are a Business Issues Worksheet and a Performance Improvement Planner.

Andre Adams, a training director at XYZ Corporation, used the strategic needs assessment approach to develop a long-term performance improvement plan for the company. XYZ Corporation is a large wholesale distributor of electronic goods. With over $3 billion in assets, the company markets a variety of products, including computers, television and video equipment, and cameras, to Far Eastern countries.

The Need

The electronics division of XYZ had not been keeping pace with its other store divisions or with its competition. Sales targets had not been met for two years. The division had been, and could again be, a very lucrative operation for the store. Management wanted to know what was causing a drop in sales and what actions, if any, were needed to turn things around.

The Approach

The training director used a five-phase approach to conduct the strategic needs assessment.

Phase 1: Assess current situation

1. The HRD director conducted a series of interviews with the president, two senior vice presidents, and a representative sampling of middle managers and first-line supervisors of the electronics division.

2. The HRD director reviewed one hundred customer-satisfaction surveys taken during the period just before sales began to drop off, then reviewed another one hundred surveys taken during the period when sales went into decline.

3. The HRD director established preliminary performance improvement goals based on system capabilities and prepared a report that summarized the key findings from the first two steps.

Phase 2: Examine External Environment

1. The HRD director researched the business environment in which XYZ and its competitors operated. This was background for a more detailed examination of the consumer electronics market. He consulted industry and trade journals and reviewed customer-satisfaction surveys.

2. He also conducted focus groups with a sample of the division's customers. As a result of these inquiries, the training director learned that much of the customer dissatisfaction resulted from a new Asian competitor who was offering lower prices and longer credit periods to his organization's current and potential customers. The competitor also delivered products faster.

Phase 3: Examine Internal Environment

1. The business plan was reviewed for its applicability to the changing environment. It revealed that the division had planned to emphasize quality and speed of delivery rather than lower prices. This plan was being executed despite the fact that the new competitor's low price policy was hurting sales. Figure 7.9 shows the business issues for XYZ Corporation.

2. Process maps for shipping and purchasing were created, and performance gaps between ideal and actual were identified.

Phase 4: Chart Future Environment

1. The senior leaders of the company and the training director identified the performance needed to regain lost market share. They decided to ask the division to emphasize quality and speed by reducing product defects and the time required to ship orders. They also decided to cut costs and extend credit and to work with the division to place greater emphasis on customer relationships.
2. A reorganization of the shipping and purchasing departments was included in the new plan, which called for improved relationships with wholesalers and distributors.

Phase 5: Develop Performance Improvement Plan

1. To ensure that the plan would be implemented smoothly, the HRD director first assessed the organization's readiness for change.
2. Based on that analysis, the following major performance-improvement projects were identified:

   • Implement a new order-management system.
   • Train to support the implementation of the new order-management system, including team building, relationship management, and customer-service training.

Figure 7.10 shows the performance-improvement planner that was used for this project.

Key business issues	Reduce order delivery time
	Develop new order-management system
	Improve linkage between shipping, receiving, and product delivery
	Improve quality of service to customers
	Improve supplier relationships
	Create ownership in order delivery process
	Reduce prices
	Extend credit period
Length problems existed	2 years
Consequences of not solving problems	Lose even more customers
Business processes affected	Shipping, sales, purchasing, credit, finance, marketing
Performance improvement goals	Reduce order delivery time by 50 percent
	Reduce product costs by 10 percent
	Extend credit by 30 days
Obstacles to success	Inability of suppliers to ship goods from overseas on time
	Union rules
	Limit on number of hours shipping and receiving personnel will work on the job

FIGURE 7.9 *Business Issues: XYZ Corporation*

The Results

The new order-management system was fully implemented one year later. It helped boost the electronics division's sales. XYZ Corporation regained the market share it had lost. A follow-up survey showed that customer-satisfaction levels were as high as they had been before the new competitor had captured some of the market.

Project Identification Number: 123

Project Description: Order delivery performance improvement

Project Sponsor (Name/Business Unit): Chuck Brady/Sales

Performance Improvement Goal: Reduce order delivery time from twenty days to ten days.

Critical Success Factors:

1. Participation of purchasing, shipping, and sales units

2. Communication of program benefits to customers and employees

3. Pilot program in two regions before nationwide rollout

Obstacles to Success:

1. Current shipping vendor's performance

2. Union rules

3. Aging inventory computer system

4. Lack of performance measures for purchasing and shipping supervisors

Prerequisites for Starting the Project:

1. Improved understanding of customer needs

2. Shipping vendor participation in sales planning

Project Structure: Steering committee composed of unit heads from purchasing, shipping, and sales; project manager; and one analyst from each business unit who understands the processes.

Team Requirements: Knowledge of policies in unit; two years' experience in purchasing, shipping, and sales process; operating knowledge of computer system

Resources: Budget, staff

Expected Cost: $1.2M

FIGURE 7.10 *Performance Improvement Planner: XYZ Corporation*

Benefits

1. Improved sales: $2.0M

2. Reduced returns: $1.0M

3. Reduced inventory: $2.0M

Timeline

Milestone	Expected Start Date	Expected Completion Date
1. Analysis	1/1	2/28
2. Cost-benefit analysis	3/1	3/5
3. Plan pilot	3/6	3/15
4. Perform pilot	3/16	3/31
5. Launch program	4/1	4/15
6. Rollout program	4/16	4/30

Completed By: _____   Approved By: _____

Date: _____   Date: _____

FIGURE 7.10 *Performance Improvement Planner: XYZ Corporation* (continued)

CONCLUSION

A strategic needs assessment addresses the needs that are linked to the core business strategies of an organization. It should be used whenever performance needs affect strategic business processes.

The success of a performance-improvement initiative depends on several factors, including an assessment of the organization's readiness to change and a carefully crafted performance-improvement plan. In this chapter we have provided ways to examine factors in the external and internal environments that can affect the organization's performance. The focus was on the organization and its processes. The next section describes strategies for managing a needs assessment project.

III

Managing a Needs Assessment

EIGHT Writing Proposals and Reports

PURPOSE

This chapter will enable you to accomplish the following:

- Explore the process of contracting a needs assessment.

- Review the purposes of a needs assessment proposal.

- Apply practical tips for writing a needs assessment proposal.

- Use the needs assessment checklist.

- Learn how to use the needs assessment proposal, the in-process reports, and the final report to manage the needs assessment.

- Learn how to manage needs assessment documents.

RELATED TOOLKIT JOB AIDS

- Needs Assessment Checklist

- Needs Assessment Proposal Worksheet

- Needs Assessment Report Worksheet

OVERVIEW

Managing a needs assessment project begins with the first client meeting and ends when the client accepts the final report. With practical project-management skills, a needs assessment can be completed efficiently and in a way that builds goodwill among those who participate. Regardless of which needs assessment approach or model you select, you should consider how you will contract the needs assessment, manage documents, and report progress.

Tip

Working on a poorly managed needs assessment feels like following a runaway train. You may not know where the train is going, but you can sure monitor its progress by following the billowing steam, hot air, damage, and destruction.

CONTRACTING A NEEDS ASSESSMENT

Contracting is the first and most critical step in the consulting process. It includes meeting with the client for the first time, writing the proposal, and obtaining the contract. A needs assessment contract is an agreement that specifies the desired outcomes or processes, the timeline, what each party will do, and the budget for a project.

Block (2000) defined a consultant as someone who has influence in a situation but does not have the power to make changes or implement programs directly. Most analysts, whether they are hired from outside or work internally, are consultants. They report to a client or decision maker who has the authority to make decisions that address the sensed need.

During their first meeting, the analyst and the client size each other up. They decide if they really want to work together, and they consider the best ways to accomplish the needs assessment. Indeed, this meeting is like a job interview. Usually, the first meeting between the analyst and the client centers on the following concerns:

- The nature of the sensed problem
- The context surrounding the problem
- The resources that various stakeholders, including the client and the analyst, bring to the project
- The timeframe for the effort

The client wants to know if the analyst has a strong work ethic, a track record of producing the expected results in similar situations, the competencies required to complete the project, and the skills to limit the costs by applying efficient methods. Implementing an effective needs assessment requires many competencies (International Board of Standards for Training, Performance, and Instruction®, 2005; King, 1998; Rothwell, 1996) including:

- Knowledge about the work environment
- Knowledge about performance improvement, management, and systems thinking
- Skill in consulting, problem-solving, negotiating, and advocating for change
- Skill in collecting data using such methods as focus groups, interviews, and observation
- Skill in analyzing qualitative and quantitative data
- Skill in exchanging information verbally, in writing, and through presentations
- Ability to collaborate effectively with the client and the project stakeholders
- Knowledge and skills in applying relevant needs assessment theories and models
- Ability to manage the needs assessment project effectively
- Ability to negotiate outcomes that maximize performance and learning

- Knowledge of ethical standards and skills in following these standards

The analyst must also consider whether the needs assessment is likely to be successful. Key questions that the analyst should answer before agreeing to implement a needs assessment include the following:

- Can the project use his or her knowledge, skills, and abilities?

- Does the client seek information for making decisions and taking action, or is the needs assessment window dressing for decisions that have already been made?

- Does the decision maker have the power to take action based on needs assessment information?

- Do all those who are involved support change?

- Do the client and project stakeholders act ethically?

- Are sufficient resources available to complete the project?

When answers to any of these questions reveal that issues exist, consider ways to address them before agreeing to conduct the needs assessment. Some additional potential obstacles and tips for overcoming them are shown in Figure 8.1.

If possible, avoid conducting a needs assessment when there are insufficient resources, the timeline is too short, the decision maker lacks the authority to take action based on the project findings, or unethical behaviors are promoted. If you cannot avoid the project, check out the consulting strategies suggested by Block (2000) and McNamara (2005) for ways to minimize the problems.

Following are some common potential needs assessment obstacles ("O") and their suggested solutions ("S").

O   Lack of consensus about goals.

S   Gain consensus by obtaining the commitment of a senior executive and communicating that commitment throughout the organization.

S   Gain consensus by convening an advisory group consisting of a senior executive, a midlevel manager, and members of the target group.

S   Revisit the business goals of the organization and ensure that the assessment ties in with one or more goals.

O   Senior management supports the effort, but line managers or supervisors do not.

S   Obtain buy-in from a line manager or supervisor who can influence other managers.

S   Seek the intervention of senior management and make the assessment a priority for middle managers.

O   Lack of a sponsor with authority.

S   Seek the support of someone in a higher position.

O   Too much background information to review in a reasonable time.

S   Revisit the goals of the assessment, establish priorities, and discard information that is not relevant to the assessment.

S   Enlist one or more groups within the organization to summarize the critical information for you.

O   Conflict about types of data that must be collected.

S   Revisit the goals of the assessment.

S   Convene an advisory group, as described earlier, to review the data collection plan and resolve the conflicts.

O   Bias in favor of a particular instrument.

S   Show the benefits of other instruments.

FIGURE 8.1 *Potential Needs Assessment Obstacles and Tips for Overcoming Them*

O   Resistance to questioning from middle management or special interest groups (such as union members or line staff).
S   Promote awareness about the benefits of the assessment through informational meetings.

S   Seek the intervention of senior management and make the assessment a priority for middle managers.
S   Explain the needs assessment process and how the results will be used.

O   Lack of access to those working night shifts or people assigned to restricted work areas.
S   Find alternative personnel.
S   Obtain special permission to gather data.

O   Disagreement among team members about the method to use to implement the assessment.
S   Seek the opinion of a third party such as a senior manager.

O   Lack of willingness on the part of people to change when implementing a new system or technology.
S   Create a change readiness program.

O   Attitude of "Who has the time to complete another survey?"
S   Obtain buy-in by having the president of the company or a senior manager endorse the process.
S   Explain benefits to users.
S   Offer incentives for completing the instrument.

O   Lack of buy-in to needs assessment results (especially negative or controversial findings).
S   Present alternatives to overcome negative or controversial findings.
S   Present "negative" findings as opportunities for improvement.

FIGURE 8.1 *Potential Needs Assessment Obstacles and Tips for Overcoming Them* (continued)

During the first client meeting, the analyst also gathers information to use in drafting a written proposal. For example, the analyst records precisely the client's description of the need, including the words and phrases that are used to describe the context, the stakeholders' roles, and the prob-

Tip

When contracting, if your gut feels queasy or the hair on the back of your neck stands up, consider whether you want to be involved in the needs assessment and whether the planned action is really appropriate, and at the same time, check the ethical guidelines in Chapter Nine.

lems or opportunities. After the analyst and the client verbally decide that a written proposal is warranted, the analyst may request copies of organization documents that are relevant to the project, including the mission statement, the strategic plan, marketing materials, organization charts, annual reports, project descriptions, and financial information. These documents provide important terms, concepts, and information about how the needs assessment fits with other organizational efforts; all of these may be included in the proposal.

Some clients prefer that the needs assessment be billed at an hourly rate, while others prefer that the consultant quote a cost for the entire project in the proposal. In the latter case, the consultant should carefully consider specifics about what will be required to complete the project. Toolkit Form 8.1 is a checklist for thinking about the important aspects of gathering preliminary data, planning the needs assessment, collecting data, analyzing the information, preparing the report, and making the presentation. Figure 8.2 lists four of the questions appearing in the Toolkit.

Tip

To obtain written records that show the correct spellings of stakeholders' names and their current titles, exchange business cards. You can encourage others to share their business cards by passing out your own card when introducing yourself.

Gather Preliminary Data
1. Have you had preliminary meetings to gather information from your client contact and other key people?
2. Have you considered the ethical guidelines that may be important in gathering and analyzing preliminary data?
3. Have you obtained senior management's perspectives about the goals of the assessment?
4. Have you identified the attitudes of learners' and other stakeholders toward the needs assessment and the new program, system, training, or technology?

FIGURE 8.2 *Some Questions from Toolkit 8.1: Needs Assessment Checklist*

THE NEEDS ASSESSMENT PROPOSAL

The needs assessment proposal is a document that offers the consultant's insights on the project's purpose, phases, processes, expected outcomes, timeline, and expenses. At the beginning of a needs assessment, the proposal to some extent frames an ambiguous situation and presents a plan of action for completing the proposed project. It also establishes the tone of the project—for example, that the project will be a collaborative effort among the client, the analyst, and the stakeholders—and clarifies responsibilities. Figure 8.3 shows a sample needs assessment proposal. (See Toolkit Form 8.2 in the Toolkit section of the book for a template.)

After the proposal is drafted, the client and the analyst review it together to ensure that the analyst has accurately understood the sensed problem and the context, and that the planned process for completing the needs assessment is appropriate and achievable. Often the client and analyst revise the initial proposal to reflect their negotiations on exactly how a needs assessment will be implemented. Most misunderstandings at this point can be negotiated. This review may occur in person, by telephone, or online. Once the proposal is approved by the client, it serves as a written contract.

Draft Proposal:
Needs Assessment for T & J Marine Products

Submitted to: Tom Sloboth
                      Plant Manager
                      T & J Marine Products
                      Street
                      City, State, Zip
                      Phone number/e-mail address

Submitted by: Sally Burns
                      Human Resource Development Consultant
                      Address
                      City, State, Zip
                      Phone number/e-mail address

Date: XX/XX/XXXX

FIGURE 8.3 *Draft Needs Assessment Proposal: T & J Marine Products*

Purpose

T & J Marine Products (T&J's) manufactures and markets products for water sports and pleasure boating. The plant is not meeting its strategic goals of increasing market leadership in two areas: developing new products and implementing new product distribution systems. The plant manager believes that a lack of supervisory knowledge and skills are likely contributors to the failure.

The needs assessment will accomplish the following:

1. Determine if, when, where, and how a lack of supervisory knowledge and skills affects workplace performance.
2. Prioritize the supervisory training that is needed to meet the strategic goals.

The needs assessment has five phases. The table on the next page shows each project phase, the purpose of the phase, the process for completing the phase, the expected outcomes, and the projected due date. Upon completion of each phase, the analyst and the plant manager will review a draft report that details the process and outcomes. They will also review the proposed processes for completing the entire needs assessment. All data collection will be completed on-site; however, all data analysis and report writing will be completed off-site. The analyst will group the data; no individual data will be reported. Note that this needs assessment focuses on knowledge and skill needs. Consequently, if Phase 1 of the project, *Gather preliminary data about the sensed needs,* reveals that a lack of knowledge and skills does not contribute significantly to the performance problem, the needs assessment will be redesigned or discontinued.

Staffing

Sally Burns, the consultant for this project, is a certified performance technologist. She has worked with many organizations to address their learning and performance needs. She subscribes to the ethical guidelines of ISPI and the Academy of Human Resource Development. She recognizes that training and non-training solutions can contribute to improved performance. She also values participation in the needs assessment by all those who may be affected by the solutions.

Cost

The costs are $150 per hour. The firm will reimburse the analyst for such agreed-upon expenses as travel and copying. The firm will also provide administrative assistance for scheduling interviews and observations, and a work station for the duration of the project. This contract may be renegotiated at any time as needed.

FIGURE 8.3 *Draft Needs Assessment Proposal: T & J Marine Products* (continued)

Table of Needs Assessment Phases, Processes, Outcomes, and Timelines

	Phase 1: Gather preliminary data about the sensed needs	Phase 2: Plan the needs assessment	Phase 3: Analyze knowledge and skill requirements	Phase 4: Analyze the data	Phase 5: Prepare the final report
Purpose	• Establish goals • Determine whether and how the lack of supervisory knowledge and skills affects T&J	• Develop a work plan to ensure that the assessment stays on target	• Develop the assessment tools and collect the assessment data	• Interpret the collected data using systematic and useful processes	• Document the needs assessment process and outcomes
Process	• Review organization, performance, and industry data • Interview two managers, two supervisors, and the human resource development director • Summarize each interview and review the summary	• Review the process for this phase and revise if needed • Determine what types of data must be collected and the sources of data • Determine the types of data-collection tools that will be used • Determine the types of analyses that	• Review the process for this phase and revise if needed • Prepare each assessment tool • Validate, pilot-test, and obtain approval for each tool from the HRD director and the plant manager • Review the	• Review the process for this phase and revise if needed • Compile the qualitative data (for example, the stories) • Compile the quantitative data (for example, survey results) • Write the	• Review the process for this phase and revise if needed • Combine information from all phases of the needs assessment • Meet with management to report the needs assessment results • Meet with supervisors

FIGURE 8.3 *Draft Needs Assessment Proposal: T & J Marine Products* (continued)

Table of Needs Assessment Phases, Processes, Outcomes, and Timelines (continued)

	Phase 1: Gather preliminary data about the sensed needs	Phase 2: Plan the needs assessment	Phase 3: Analyze knowledge and skill requirements	Phase 4: Analyze the data	Phase 5: Prepare the final report
	document with the interviewee	must be performed • Decide how data will be collected and managed	draft data-collection process with those who will be involved in it and revise the process based on their feedback • Collect the data • Monitor the data-collection process • Organize the data	draft analysis • Draft the training priorities • Meet with the plant manager to review the draft analysis • Meet with those who will be affected to review the draft analysis	to report the needs assessment results
Outcome	A draft report that (1) summarizes the archival data reviewed and the interviews, (2) establishes goals for the assessment, and (3) describes whether and how lack of	A draft report that recommends (1) the type of data to be collected, (2) the data sources, (3) the types of data-collection tools to be used, (4) the types of analysis to be	A draft report that (1) documents the needs assessment tools and describes the validation, pilot testing, and approval processes, (2) describes the meeting to	A draft report of the analyzed data and training priorities that is disseminated to those who are involved in the process	The final needs assessment report

FIGURE 8.3 *Draft Needs Assessment Proposal: T & J Marine Products* (continued)

**Table of Needs Assessment Phases, Processes,
Outcomes, and Timelines** (continued)

Phase 1: Gather preliminary data about the sensed needs	Phase 2: Plan the needs assessment	Phase 3: Analyze knowledge and skill requirements	Phase 4: Analyze the data	Phase 5: Prepare the final report
supervisory skills affects T&J's performance and whether the solution should include training, and (4) identifies non-training solutions that could contribute to performance improvement	performed, and (5) how the collected data will be managed	review the data-collection process with stakeholders and any revisions to the process, and (3) describes how data were collected, monitored, and organized for analysis		
Projected Due Date	April 3	April 19	May 17	June 2	June 9

FIGURE 8.3 *Draft Needs Assessment Proposal: T & J Marine Products* (continued)

Tip

Before reviewing the draft proposal with a client, the analyst can state that changes in the document are expected. Normally, the client and analyst together identify a few terms or steps in the process that require clarification. The client's revisions to the proposal indicate his or her commitment to the project. When the draft proposal is revised, be sure to include these edits.

Ways to Use the Needs Assessment Proposal

A written needs assessment proposal serves many purposes. As previously described, it initially frames the project and, once approved, serves as a written contract for the needs assessment.

Project creep occurs when the scope of a project keeps growing. *Project shrink* occurs when the scope of the project keeps getting smaller. To prevent either situation, use the approved proposal to guide the needs assessment process. For example, complete the needs assessment in phases. Immediately before beginning a phase, review with the client the process that was documented in the approved proposal. After each phase, set the stage for obtaining client approval of the interim report for the phase by reviewing the approved proposal. As conditions change in organizations, such reviews can prevent wasted efforts.

The approved needs assessment proposal also serves as a communication tool. For example, the analyst can share a copy of it with interviewees and use the table as a visual map to show how individual contributions fit into the larger project.

In addition, the approved needs assessment proposal provides a record of the project's decisions. As such it serves as the benchmark for in-process and final reports and for renegotiating the needs assessment, if necessary. The proposal is not written in stone; it should be renegotiated as expectations shift. Of course, such renegotiations may affect the project's outcomes, costs, and timeline.

Practical Tips for Writing a Needs Assessment Proposal

Following are some practical tips for writing a needs assessment proposal:

- The cover page should contain the project name, the client's name and contact information, the analyst's name and contact information, and the date. If you have ever dug through a pile of papers on your desk to find important information about a project, you will realize the importance and convenience of having contact information on the cover page.

- Check and double-check spelling, especially proper nouns and organization-specific terms.

- Write the proposal in business language. Use organization-specific language and keep to the point. Most needs assessment proposals for business are three to six pages, but there are times when a longer proposal is needed.

- In the purpose section, remind the reader why the project is important and the value of the expected accomplishment.

- Because most problems require both training and non-training solutions, consider addressing both training and non-training in the needs assessment proposal. Do so in a way that considers the analyst's skills and that works for the client and the organization. (Note: this often requires conferring with the client.)

- Verify budgetary constraints so that recommendations are reasonable and on target.

- Place the cost section at the end of the document so the client sees it after he or she understands how the needs assessment is framed and the plans for completing it.

- Document each revision to a needs assessment proposal in writing and date the document. (This document can be referred to if a new client joins the project or if any disagreement later arises about the project.)

- Number the pages of the proposal, and staple or bind the proposal if sending a paper copy.

A proposal that is accepted or approved by the client becomes the contract for the needs assessment. To protect both the client and the analyst, it is usually best to document this agreement in writing. With the contract in place, the analyst can focus on completing each phase of the needs assessment in turn.

MANAGING NEEDS ASSESSMENT DOCUMENTS

A quick review of the table in Figure 8.3, the draft needs assessment proposal, reveals that every phase involves collecting, analyzing, and synthesizing data. Consequently, the number of documents that the analyst uses and creates can become overwhelming unless they are organized and well managed, especially in a large needs assessment. To avoid losing information that is irreplaceable and wasting time thumbing through documents to find just the right one, analysts create a project management system and routinely organize needs assessment information as it is collected.

Most needs assessment projects include digital documents (such as electronic reports) and printed documents (such as company brochures and business cards), so the project management systems should accommodate both types of documents. A project management system should include a physical folder for each of the following elements:

- Contact information (such as business cards)
- Background information
- Each phase of the project
- Project notes
- Budget and cost information
- Miscellaneous information
- Computer back-up discs

It should also contain electronic folders for background materials, reports, collected data, and analyzed data. Having organized locations for all needs assessment materials and reports and back-up copies of computer files makes it easier to write reports and saves hours of work. An inexpensive file box works well for storing such materials: it keeps everything together in one place and does not take up much space in the office. Furthermore, it is portable, so project materials can be available at meetings.

Reports

A needs assessment project typically relies on in-process reports and a final report. An in-process report documents the purpose, process, outcomes, and timeline for one phase of the needs assessment. The final report may be a compilation of the proposal and all the in-process reports, together with a brief introduction. (Alternative forms of reporting can be found in Torres, Preskill, and Piontek, 2005.)

The client and other stakeholders review these reports and provide feedback that keeps the needs assessment project on track. Equally important, the process of reviewing reports engages stakeholders in the needs assessment process, which facilitates later implementation of its solutions.

Tip A needs assessment report highlights some aspects of a situation and minimizes other aspects. Think carefully about what you highlight and minimize!

To draft an in-process report quickly, use the table in the approved proposal. Use your word processing program to copy and paste the selected column from the table into a new document. Revise the text to reflect what actually occurred, add a cover page, and format the document. Figure 8.4 shows an in-process draft report for Phase 1 of the T & J Marine Products Needs Assessment.

Most needs assessment projects also require a final report. If you have been providing interim reports and maintaining contact with the client,

Draft Report
Needs Assessment for T & J Marine Products
Phase 1: Gather preliminary data about the sensed needs

Submitted to: Tom Sloboth
Plant Manager
T & J Marine Products
Street
City, State, Zip
Phone number/e-mail address

Submitted by: Sally Burns
Human Resource Development Consultant
Address
City, State, Zip
Phone number/e-mail address

Date: XX/XX/XXXX

FIGURE 8.4 *Phase 1 In-Process Report for T & J Marine Products*

Executive Summary

This first phase of the needs assessment gathered preliminary data about the sensed needs. The outcomes of this phase provide the foundation for Phase 2 of the needs assessment. The goals, process, findings, and recommendations for this phase are summarized here.

Goals:

1. To establish goals for the assessment
2. Determine whether and how the lack of supervisory knowledge and skills affects T&J's performance.

Process:

The needs assessment process for this phase included the following steps:

1. Review organizational, performance, and industry data.
2. Interview two managers, two supervisors, and the human resource development director.
3. Summarize each interview and review the document with the interviewee.

Findings:

1. The market for water sports and pleasure boating is changing. To compete effectively, T&J must meet its strategic goals.
2. Lack of consistent processes and walking the talk by upper management caused some lack of trust.
3. Interviewees recognized that the boating industry has become more competitive, and they wanted more timely information to use in improving their performance.
4. Some interviewees are competent in telling managers what they want to hear rather than in reporting the actual situation.
5. Supervisors need additional knowledge and skills to achieve the strategic goals.
6. Non-training needs that should be addressed to improve performance include improving feedback from managers and improving work processes by eliminating unnecessary process steps.

Recommendations: The Phase 1 results indicate that for T&J to achieve its strategic goals, the supervisors need new knowledge and skills. To improve performance most effectively, non-training needs should be addressed at the same time.

FIGURE 8.4 *Phase 1 In-Process Report for T & J Marine Products* (continued)

Phase 1: Gather preliminary data about the sensed needs

Goal

The goal of this first phase of the project was twofold:

1. To establish goals for the assessment
2. To obtain a broad understanding of whether and how the lack of supervisory knowledge and skills affects T&J's performance and whether the solution should include training (See Attachment A: *Projected Needs Assessment Phases, Processes, Outcomes, and Timelines.*)

Process

Completing this phase of the needs assessment involved the following steps:

1. Review organizational, performance, and industry data.
2. Interview two managers, two supervisors, and the human resource development director.
3. Summarize each interview and review the document with the interviewee.

Step 1: Review organizational, performance, and industry data

To complete this step, the following organizational data were reviewed:

- Strategic plan
- Organization chart
- Marketing reports for product areas
- Product development plan
- Product distribution plan
- T&J's culture survey results for 2005 and 2006

The following performance data were reviewed:

- The performance reports for each unit

The following industry data were reviewed:
  For the boating industry:

- *Boating Industry* (magazine) annual statistical review
- Recreational Boat Building Industry home page: http://www.rbbi.com

  For water sports:

- www.roho.co.uk
- www.boothandel.nl
- www.nauticfriend.com

FIGURE 8.4 *Phase 1 In-Process Report for T & J Marine Products* (continued)

Step 2: Interview a manager, two supervisors, and the human resource development director

The analyst conducted interviews between April 6 and April 10 with two managers, two supervisors, and the HRD director. The analyst chose these interviewees on the basis of their key roles in contributing to the organization's strategic goals. The analyst began each interview with a short introduction about the purpose of the needs assessment, and a discussion about how the interviewee was chosen to participate in the needs assessment and how their information would be used. Each interviewee was told that information would be grouped for reporting and that only triangulated information (that is, information that was obtained from more than one person or one data-collection method) would be reported.

Notes were taken during each interview. They were also digitally recorded as a back-up.

Step 3: Summarize each interview and review the document with the interviewee

After the analyst summarized the interviews and excerpted key facts, each interviewee reviewed the text of his or her interview and noted points of clarification or modification. The interviews were revised to reflect these changes.

Phase 1 Findings

The preliminary data reported in this section were obtained from at least two people or by at least two data-collection methods.

1. The market for water sports and pleasure boating is changing. To compete effectively, T&J must meet its strategic goals.
2. Lack of consistent processes and walking the talk by upper management caused some lack of trust.
3. Interviewees recognized that the boating industry has become more competitive, and they wanted more timely information to use in improving their performance.
4. Some interviewees are competent in telling managers what they want to hear rather than in reporting the actual situation.
5. Supervisors need additional knowledge and skills to achieve the strategic goals.
6. Non-training needs that should be addressed to improve performance include improving feedback from managers and improving work processes by eliminating unnecessary process steps.

Recommendations

The Phase 1 results indicate that for T&J to achieve its strategic goals, the supervisors need new knowledge and skills. One example is to understand the strategic performance reports. The outcomes of this phase provide the foundation for Phase 2 of the needs assessment. To improve performance most effectively, non-training needs should be addressed at the same time.

FIGURE 8.4 *Phase 1 In-Process Report for T & J Marine Products* (continued)

the final report with its findings and recommendations will not come as a surprise. The following items may be included in a formal report:

- Executive summary (typically a page)
- Purpose
- Process
- Findings
- Recommendations
- Appendix (including supporting instruments and data)

When preparing reports, include pie charts, graphs, and diagrams as appropriate to highlight key findings.

In-Person Oral Reports and Presentations

In-person oral reports and presentations provide an opportunity for the client and other stakeholders to ask questions, discuss the findings, and consider the implications of the needs assessment. In other words, such reports and presentations provide a forum that enables the needs assessment stakeholders to *own the results.* The final report is the basis for discussion during the final meeting on the needs assessment. It documents both the needs assessment process and findings.

Report the positives that you found in the situation first. Report your findings about potential improvements honestly and in a way that respects all the stakeholders. Identify problem areas cited by multiple sources, and recommend one or more feasible actions.

Following are guidelines for these presentations:

- Tailor the presentation style to the culture of the organization and to the decision makers' preferences. Today, many oral presentations rely on PowerPoint slides, but check with the client before preparing the presentation. Avoid the mistake made by the consultant who presented a group of decision makers in a fast-paced organization with a fifty-page report. That consultant, after spending many hours writing the report, was disappointed when nobody read it.

- Use a cost-benefit analysis when appropriate (for an overview of how to do a cost-benefit analysis, see Phillips, 2003; Swanson & Gradous, 1990).

- Structure the meeting to move from the known and easy to the unknown and more difficult. Use the needs assessment proposal to remind everyone about the situation at the start of the needs assessment.

- Recognize that some people may want to edit the report. If their edits are fitting, accept them. If their edits are problematic, you may need to explain why you did not include them in your report.

- Support your recommendations with citations from authorities in the field and your knowledge of industry best practices.

Tip
Hale (2005) pointed out that performance improvement professionals often cram their language and models into the clients' head. While as experts we need to know the professional ideas, language, and models, Hale advised that when we work with clients we should avoid using our jargon and as much as possible talk to clients in their own language.

CONCLUSION

Managing the needs assessment process is essential to completing the project effectively and in a timely manner. Most needs assessments are not implemented exactly as they are proposed and must be modified. For example, an interviewee may be on vacation during the time for data collection or a new decision maker may join the project and wish to make changes. Manage the needs assessment process to allow for flexibility, stakeholder input, and progress, and thus increase the probability that the client will use the needs assessment findings. The next chapter focuses on ethics, which can also influence how needs assessment projects are conducted and how findings are used.

NINE Ethical Issues

PURPOSE

This chapter will enable you to do the following:

- Examine ethical issues relevant to needs assessments.

- Refer to ethical standards used by several different professional organizations.

OVERVIEW

In this chapter, we focus on an area where expert-level insights are critical—the ethical issues that sometimes arise during a needs assessment. We introduce some ethical issues for consideration and present ethical guidelines (which are sometimes called standards) that have been adopted by various professional organizations. By having these standards available, you can refer to them as ethical issues arise.

ETHICS IN NEEDS ASSESSMENT

Most decisions in a needs assessment involve value judgments, and value judgments often lead to ethical issues. Because a needs assessment is built on the trust of everyone who participates, your personal integrity and your ability to negotiate skillfully such issues as confidentiality, conflict of interest, data representation, and so forth are critical to achieving a successful needs assessment and the later implementation of your recommendations.

> **Case**
>
> Ethical issues in needs assessment are often linked. For example, when the U.S. Centers for Disease Control and Prevention (CDC) collects needs assessment data for HIV-prevention programs, they must protect the confidentiality of individuals who contacted counselors to be tested on whether they are infected with the HIV virus. Simultaneously the CDC must ensure that the agency collects accurate data on the rate of HIV transmission for decision making. Although it is difficult, the needs assessment should be designed to address the ethical issues related to confidentiality, respect for patients' rights, and data accuracy. In this case, CDC must assure client accuracy without using client names.

Knowing your personal and professional values before you start a needs assessment is helpful in establishing and managing others' expectations about how you will act in specific situations. Figure 9.1 presents examples of issues that have arisen in actual needs assessments. As you read them, consider how well you know your own personal and professional values.

> **Tip**
>
> Most needs assessments are by nature political because they involve either support for or challenges to those who are in power. In such situations, ethics are likely to be important.

Ethical Issues or Not; You Decide.

As you read each of the following real-life scenarios, decide whether ethical issues are involved and what appropriate actions you could take.

- During a random review of organization documents, you discover that a manager has downloaded child pornography from the Internet.

- Your client guesses the name of an interviewee who made negative comments in a confidential interview. She plans to "correct the person's misperceptions."

- A person on the needs assessment team misrepresents the data in hopes of influencing an external agency to fund developmental activities that she believes will be beneficial for the agency.

- A colleague asks to use the job and task data you are collecting to negotiate a higher salary.

- While conducting a competency analysis for a division, the firm's president tells you confidentially that the division will be shut down and that your client (the HR manager), who does not yet know this information, will be laid off.

- The well-known instrument your team uses to determine needs for individual development and education is not valid, but clients really like the results and find them useful.

- You realize that your client's goal for the needs assessment is to provide objective data that will support his department's claim for an increased share of the organization's budget.

FIGURE 9.1 *Examples of Real-Life Needs Assessment Issues*

Individuals who are working on a needs assessment may find it difficult to sort out the ethical issues in a situation and to identify appropriate responses to them. In recent years, professional associations have developed guidelines, or standards, that help in identifying and negotiating ethical issues. Such guidelines can be found at the following Web sites:

- Joint Committee on Standards for Educational Evaluation, Program Evaluation Standards: http://www.wmich.edu/evalctr/jc

- American Evaluation Association, Guiding Principles for Evaluators: http://www.eval.org/Publications/GuidingPrinciples.asp

- International Society for Performance Improvement, Human Performance Technology Code of Ethics: http://www.ispi.org

- Academy of Human Resource Development, Standards on Ethics and Integrity: http://www.ahrd.org

- American Psychological Association, Ethical Principles of Psychologists and Code of Conduct: http://www.apa.org/ethics/code2002.html

- Organization Development Network, Principles of Practice: http://www.odnetwork.org/principlesofpractice.html

As you look at the guidelines at these sites and at the several sets of standards and the background on their development discussed here, note their similarities and differences.

Joint Committee on Standards for Educational Evaluation, Program Evaluation Standards

In 1975, twelve professional organizations that had concerns about the conduct of evaluations (including needs assessments) formed the Joint Committee on Standards for Educational Evaluation. This committee continues to be located at the Evaluation Center at Western Michigan University. They issued their first set of standards in 1981, revolving around four areas:

- Utility
- Feasibility
- Propriety
- Accuracy

A second edition of these standards was published in 1994, and they are still considered current. The standards are shown in Figure 9.2.

The Program Evaluation Standards
Summary of the Standards

Utility Standards

The utility standards are intended to ensure that an evaluation will serve the information needs of intended users.

U1 Stakeholder Identification—Persons involved in or affected by the evaluation should be identified so that their needs can be addressed.

U2 Evaluator Credibility—The persons conducting the evaluation should be both trustworthy and competent to perform the evaluation so that the evaluation findings achieve maximum credibility and acceptance.

U3 Information Scope and Selection—Information collected should be broadly selected to address pertinent questions about the program and be responsive to the needs and interests of clients and other specified stakeholders.

U4 Values Identification—The perspectives, procedures, and rationale used to interpret the findings should be carefully described so that the bases for value judgments are clear.

U5 Report Clarity—Evaluation reports should clearly describe the program being evaluated, including its context, and the purposes, procedures, and findings of the evaluation so that essential information is provided and easily understood.

U6 Report Timeliness and Dissemination—Significant interim findings and evaluation reports should be disseminated to intended users so that they can be used in a timely fashion.

U7 Evaluation Impact—Evaluations should be planned, conducted, and reported in ways that encourage follow-through by stakeholders so that the likelihood that the evaluation will be used is increased.

Feasibility Standards

The feasibility standards are intended to ensure that an evaluation will be realistic, prudent, diplomatic, and frugal.

F1 Practical Procedures—The evaluation procedures should be practical, to keep disruption to a minimum while needed information is obtained.

F2 Political Viability—The evaluation should be planned and conducted in anticipation of the different positions of various interest groups so that their

FIGURE 9.2 *Joint Committee on Standards for Educational Evaluation, Program Evaluation Standards*

Source: http://www.eval.org/EvaluationDocuments/progeval.html

cooperation may be obtained and so that possible attempts by any of these groups to curtail evaluation operations or to bias or misapply the results can be averted or counteracted.

F3 Cost Effectiveness—The evaluation should be efficient and produce information of sufficient value so that the resources expended can be justified.

Propriety Standards

The propriety standards are intended to ensure that an evaluation will be conducted legally, ethically, and with due regard for the welfare of those involved in the evaluation, as well as for those affected by its results.

P1 Service Orientation—Evaluations should be designed to assist organizations to address and effectively serve the needs of the full range of targeted participants.

P2 Formal Agreements—Obligations of the formal parties to an evaluation (what is to be done, how, by whom, and when) should be agreed to in writing so that these parties are obligated to adhere to all conditions of the agreement or formally to renegotiate it.

P3 Rights of Human Subjects—Evaluations should be designed and conducted to respect and protect the rights and welfare of human subjects.

P4 Human Interactions—Evaluators should respect human dignity and worth in their interactions with other persons associated with an evaluation so that participants are not threatened or harmed.

P5 Complete and Fair Assessment—The evaluation should be complete and fair in its examination and recording of strengths and weaknesses of the program being evaluated so that strengths can be built upon and problem areas addressed.

P6 Disclosure of Findings—The formal parties to an evaluation should ensure that the full set of evaluation findings along with pertinent limitations are made accessible to the persons affected by the evaluation, and to any others with expressed legal rights to receive the results.

P7 Conflict of Interest—Conflict of interest should be dealt with openly and honestly so that it does not compromise the evaluation processes and results.

FIGURE 9.2 *Joint Committee on Standards for Educational Evaluation, Program Evaluation Standards* (continued)

Source: http://www.eval.org/EvaluationDocuments/progeval.html

P8 Fiscal Responsibility—The evaluator's allocation and expenditure of resources should reflect sound accountability procedures and otherwise be prudent and ethically responsible so that expenditures are accounted for and appropriate.

Accuracy Standards

The accuracy standards are intended to ensure that an evaluation will reveal and convey technically adequate information about the features that determine the worth or merit of the program being evaluated.

A1 Program Documentation—The program being evaluated should be described and documented clearly and accurately so that the program is clearly identified.

A2 Context Analysis—The context in which the program exists should be examined in enough detail that its likely influences on the program can be identified.

A3 Described Purposes and Procedures—The purposes and procedures of the evaluation should be monitored and described in enough detail that they can be identified and assessed.

A4 Defensible Information Sources—The sources of information used in a program evaluation should be described in enough detail that the adequacy of the information can be assessed.

A5 Valid Information—The information gathering procedures should be chosen or developed and then implemented so that they will ensure that the interpretation arrived at is valid for the intended use.

A6 Reliable Information—The information gathering procedures should be chosen or developed and then implemented so that they will ensure that the information obtained is sufficiently reliable for the intended use.

A7 Systematic Information—The information collected, processed, and reported in an evaluation should be systematically reviewed and any errors found should be corrected.

A8 Analysis of Quantitative Information—Quantitative information in an evaluation should be appropriately and systematically analyzed so that evaluation questions are effectively answered.

FIGURE 9.2 *Joint Committee on Standards for Educational Evaluation, Program Evaluation Standards* (continued)

Source: http://www.eval.org/EvaluationDocuments/progeval.html

A9 Analysis of Qualitative Information—Qualitative information in an evaluation should be appropriately and systematically analyzed so that evaluation questions are effectively answered.

A10 Justified Conclusions—The conclusions reached in an evaluation should be explicitly justified so that stakeholders can assess them.

A11 Impartial Reporting—Reporting procedures should guard against distortion caused by personal feelings and biases of any party to the evaluation so that evaluation reports fairly reflect the evaluation findings.

A12 Meta-evaluation—The evaluation itself should be formatively and summatively evaluated against these and other pertinent standards so that its conduct is appropriately guided, and so that on completion stakeholders can closely examine its strengths and weaknesses.

FIGURE 9.2 *Joint Committee on Standards for Educational Evaluation, Program Evaluation Standards* (continued)

Source: http://www.eval.org/EvaluationDocuments/progeval.html

American Evaluation Association, Guiding Principles

Although the Joint Committee's Program Evaluation Standards already existed, members of the American Evaluation Association felt it was important for the organization to develop its own set of principles. The Guiding Principles for Evaluators focus on five major principles:

- Systematic inquiry
- Competence
- Integrity and honesty
- Respect for people
- Responsibilities for the general and public welfare

These Guiding Principles were first issued in 1995; they were reviewed and revised, and the revisions were ratified by the membership in 2004 (see Figure 9.3). Note that Principle 2 focuses on evaluation questions. In a needs assessment, the evaluation questions revolve around which needs should be addressed and the criteria for making such decisions.

The Principles

A. Systematic Inquiry: Evaluators conduct systematic, data-based inquiries.

1. To ensure the accuracy and credibility of the evaluative information they produce, evaluators should adhere to the highest technical standards appropriate to the methods they use.

2. Evaluators should explore with the client the shortcomings and strengths of both the various evaluation questions and the various approaches that might be used for answering those questions.

3. Evaluators should communicate their methods and approaches accurately and in sufficient detail to allow others to understand, interpret, and critique their work. They should make clear the limitations of an evaluation and its results. Evaluators should discuss in a contextually appropriate way those values, assumptions, theories, methods, results, and analyses significantly affecting the interpretation of the evaluative findings. These statements apply to all aspects of the evaluation, from its initial conceptualization to the eventual use of findings.

B. Competence: Evaluators provide competent performance to stakeholders.

1. Evaluators should possess (or ensure that the evaluation team possesses) the education, abilities, skills, and experience appropriate to undertake the tasks proposed in the evaluation.

2. To ensure recognition, accurate interpretation, and respect for diversity, evaluators should ensure that the members of the evaluation team collectively demonstrate cultural competence. Cultural competence would be reflected in evaluators seeking awareness of their own culturally based assumptions, their understanding of the worldviews of culturally different participants and stakeholders in the evaluation, and the use of appropriate evaluation strategies and skills in working with culturally different groups. Diversity may be in terms of race, ethnicity, gender, religion, socioeconomics, or other factors pertinent to the evaluation context.

3. Evaluators should practice within the limits of their professional training and competence, and should decline to conduct evaluations that fall substantially outside those limits. When declining the commission or request is not feasible or appropriate, evaluators should make clear any significant limitations on the evaluation that might result. Evaluators should

FIGURE 9.3 *American Evaluation Association, Guiding Principles for Evaluators*

Source: http://eval.org/Publications/GuidingPrinciples.asp

make every effort to gain the competence directly or through the assistance of others who possess the required expertise.

4. Evaluators should continually seek to maintain and improve their competencies in order to provide the highest level of performance in their evaluations. This continuing professional development might include formal coursework and workshops, self-study, evaluations of one's own practice, and working with other evaluators to learn from their skills and expertise.

C. Integrity/Honesty: Evaluators display honesty and integrity in their own behavior, and attempt to ensure the honesty and integrity of the entire evaluation process.

1. Evaluators should negotiate honestly with clients and relevant stakeholders concerning the costs, tasks to be undertaken, limitations of methodology, scope of results likely to be obtained, and uses of data resulting from a specific evaluation. It is primarily the evaluator's responsibility, not the client's, to initiate discussion and clarification of these matters.

2. Before accepting an evaluation assignment, evaluators should disclose any roles or relationships they have that might pose a conflict of interest (or appearance of a conflict) with their role as an evaluator. If they proceed with the evaluation, the conflict should be clearly articulated in reports of the evaluation results.

3. Evaluators should record all changes made in the originally negotiated project plans, and the reasons why the changes were made. If the changes would significantly affect the scope and likely results of the evaluation, the evaluator should inform the client and other important stakeholders of the changes and their likely impact in a timely fashion (barring good reason to the contrary) before proceeding with further work.

4. Evaluators should be explicit about their own, their clients,' and other stakeholders' interests and values concerning the conduct and outcomes of an evaluation.

5. Evaluators should not misrepresent their procedures, data, or findings. Within reasonable limits, they should attempt to prevent or correct misuse of their work by others.

6. If evaluators determine that certain procedures or activities are likely to produce misleading evaluative information or conclusions, they have the responsibility to communicate their concerns and the reasons for them.

FIGURE 9.3 *American Evaluation Association, Guiding Principles for Evaluators,* (continued)

Source: http://eval.org/Publications/GuidingPrinciples.asp

If discussions with the client do not resolve these concerns, the evaluator should decline to conduct the evaluation. If declining the assignment is unfeasible or inappropriate, the evaluator should consult colleagues or relevant stakeholders about other, proper ways to proceed. (Options might include discussions at a higher level, a dissenting cover letter or appendix, or refusal to sign the final document.)

7. Evaluators should disclose all sources of financial support for an evaluation, and the source of the request for the evaluation.

D. Respect for People: Evaluators respect the security, dignity, and self-worth of respondents, program participants, clients, and other evaluation stakeholders.

1. Evaluators should seek a comprehensive understanding of the important contextual elements of the evaluation. Contextual factors that may influence the results of a study include geographic location, timing, political and social climate, economic conditions, and other relevant activities in progress at the same time.

2. Evaluators should abide by current professional ethics, standards, and regulations regarding risks, harms, and burdens that might befall those participating in the evaluation; regarding informed consent for participation in evaluation; and regarding informing participants and clients about the scope and limits of confidentiality.

3. Because justified negative or critical conclusions from an evaluation must be explicitly stated, evaluations sometimes produce results that harm client or stakeholder interests. Under this circumstance, evaluators should seek to maximize the benefits and reduce any unnecessary harms that might occur, provided this will not compromise the integrity of the evaluation findings. Evaluators should carefully judge when the benefits from doing the evaluation or in performing certain evaluation procedures should be foregone because of the risks or harms. To the extent possible, these issues should be anticipated during the negotiation of the evaluation.

4. Knowing that evaluations may negatively affect the interests of some stakeholders, evaluators should conduct the evaluation and communicate its results in a way that clearly respects the stakeholders' dignity and self-worth.

FIGURE 9.3 *American Evaluation Association, Guiding Principles for Evaluators,* (continued)

Source: http://eval.org/Publications/GuidingPrinciples.asp

5. Where feasible, evaluators should attempt to foster social equity in evaluation so that those who give to the evaluation may benefit in return. For example, evaluators should seek to ensure that those who bear the burdens of contributing data and of incurring any risks do so willingly, and that they have full knowledge of and opportunity to obtain any benefits of the evaluation. Program participants should be informed that their eligibility to receive services does not hinge on their participation in the evaluation.

6. Evaluators have the responsibility to understand and respect differences among participants, such as differences in their culture, religion, gender, disability, age, sexual orientation, and ethnicity, and to account for potential implications of these differences when planning, conducting, analyzing, and reporting evaluations.

E. Responsibilities for General and Public Welfare: Evaluators articulate and take into account the diversity of general and public interests and values that may be related to the evaluation.

1. When planning and reporting evaluations, evaluators should include relevant perspectives and interests of the full range of stakeholders.

2. Evaluators should consider not only the immediate operations and outcomes of whatever is being evaluated, but also its broad assumptions, implications, and potential side effects.

3. Freedom of information is essential in a democracy. Evaluators should allow all relevant stakeholders access to evaluative information in forms that respect people and honor promises of confidentiality. Evaluators should disseminate information to stakeholders as resources allow. Communications that are tailored to a given stakeholder should include all results that may bear on interests of that stakeholder and refer to any other tailored communications to other stakeholders. In all cases, evaluators should strive to present results clearly and simply so that clients and other stakeholders can easily understand the evaluation process and results.

4. Evaluators should maintain a balance between client needs and other needs. Evaluators necessarily have a special relationship with the client who funds or requests the evaluation. By virtue of that relationship, evaluators must strive to meet legitimate client needs whenever feasible and appropriate to do so. However, that relationship can also place evaluators in difficult dilemmas when client interests conflict with other

FIGURE 9.3 *American Evaluation Association, Guiding Principles for Evaluators,* (continued)

Source: http://eval.org/Publications/GuidingPrinciples.asp

interests, or when client interests conflict with the obligation of evaluators for systematic inquiry, competence, integrity, and respect for people.
In these cases, evaluators should explicitly identify and discuss the conflicts with the client and relevant stakeholders, resolve them when possible, determine whether continued work on the evaluation is advisable if
the conflicts cannot be resolved, and make clear any significant limitations on the evaluation that might result if the conflict is not resolved.

5. Evaluators have obligations that encompass the public interest and good.
These obligations are especially important when evaluators are supported by
publicly generated funds; but clear threats to the public good should never
be ignored in any evaluation. Because the public interest and good are rarely
the same as the interests of any particular group (including those of the client
or funder), evaluators will usually have to go beyond analysis of particular
stakeholder interests and consider the welfare of society as a whole.

FIGURE 9.3 *American Evaluation Association, Guiding Principles for Evaluators,*
(continued)

Source: http://eval.org/Publications/GuidingPrinciples.asp

International Society for Performance Improvement, Code of Ethics

The next set of ethical standards was established by the International
Society for Performance Improvement (ISPI). These standards emphasize six principles of ethical practice (see Figure 9.4). ISPI's program,
Certified Performance Technologist, distinguishes practitioners who
have proven that they can produce performance improvement and training results using a systematic process. Individuals who wish to receive
this certification must sign a statement agreeing to conduct themselves
in ways that are in keeping with the six principles.

Academy of Human Resource Development, Standards on Ethics and Integrity

The primary goal of the Academy of Human Resource Development
Standards on Ethics and Integrity was to "define more clearly a holistic balance among individuals, groups, organizations, communities, and

The Code of Ethics is intended to promote ethical practice in the profession. . . . The Code of Ethics is based on six principles:

1. **Add Value Principle.** Strive to conduct yourself, and manage your projects and their results, in ways that add value for your clients, their customers, and the global environment.

2. **Validated Practice Principle.** Make use of and promote validated practices in performance technology strategies and standards.

3. **Collaboration Principle.** Work collaboratively with clients and users, functioning as a trustworthy strategic partner.

4. **Continuous Improvement Principle.** Continually improve your proficiency in the field of performance technology.

5. **Integrity Principle.** Be honest and truthful in your representations to clients, colleagues, and others with whom you may come in contact while practicing performance technology.

6. **Uphold Confidentiality Principle.** Maintain client confidentiality, not allowing for any conflict of interest that would benefit yourself or others.

FIGURE 9.4 *International Society for Performance Improvement, Code of Ethics*

Source: http://www.ispi.org

societies whenever conflicting needs arise" (Russ-Eft et al., 1999, ii). Because conflicting needs often arise when conducting a needs assessment, these standards are particularly useful. They include seven general principles plus decision rules for many situations that HRD professionals encounter, including those found in needs assessments. The standards can be accessed at www.AHRD.org.

CONCLUSION

This chapter has focused on the ethical issues you may confront when conducting a needs assessment. Various ethical issues in needs assessments might be linked. You should know your personal and professional values before engaging in a needs assessment. In addition, this chapter has presented several sets of guidelines for ethical standards and ethical practices from professional organizations. These guidelines can provide you with direction when facing difficult ethical issues.

TEN

Answers to Frequently Asked Questions

PURPOSE

This chapter will enable you to learn answers to frequently asked questions about needs assessments.

OVERVIEW

In this chapter we present answers to the questions that are commonly asked about needs assessments. You can use the answers to these commonly asked questions to improve the efficiency and effectiveness of your needs assessment projects.

COMMONLY ASKED QUESTIONS AND THEIR ANSWERS

Following are seven commonly asked questions about needs assessments and their answers.

1. Some people tell me that reports of previous needs assessment are collecting dust in their offices. How can I make sure the findings from my needs assessment are used?

Consider the following strategies for increasing the usability of your needs assessments:

- *Select projects carefully.* Before agreeing to work on a project, find out whether the proposed project addresses important performance or learning requirements. Also determine whether the project's clients and stakeholders have the needed authority, visible support for the project, and desire to take action. Determine whether the project is likely to produce findings that are relevant, timely, and useful. Examine the political context, including the level of consensus among key stakeholders. Identify potential obstacles to a successful outcome and work with your client to determine if and how they can be overcome before agreeing to conduct the needs assessment.

- *Involve the client and stakeholders in the needs assessment process in ways that are meaningful to them.* Involve them in learning and decision making regarding the needs assessment process and facilitate their participation in implementing the findings.

- *Realize that the seemingly logical process of implementing a needs assessment may actually modify the situation.* That is, the needs assessment is an intervention. During an effective needs assessment, the client and stakeholders adjust their perceptions and gain new insights. The interpersonal dynamics in the situation will often change during the data-collection and analysis process. These adjustments in perceptions, values, and power dynamics are often as powerful as the needs assessment findings that are documented in the final report.

- *Implement the needs assessment in phases and use the findings from each phase as the basis for action in the next phase,* as was illustrated in the sample needs assessment proposal in Chapter Eight.

- *Keep the needs assessment focused on the agreed-upon purpose.* Conduct regular meetings with stakeholders to review the needs assessment purpose and the current progress toward that purpose. Negotiate any proposed changes in the purpose with the client and stakeholders. Do not allow the needs assessment process to be subverted for personal gain.

  • *If the needs assessment findings were not used, explore with the client the reasons for this decision.* Determine if some of these reasons can be overcome, and ascertain whether some parts of the recommendations can be implemented.

2. How can I avoid having the needs assessment results used for actions that may create long-term problems for the organization, such as inappropriate lay-offs and downsizing?

Needs assessment findings often point to an opportunity for developing people within an organization. Some organizational leaders may, however, view the findings as an opportunity to remove individuals and reduce costs. Here are a few suggestions for avoiding this as well as other potentially inappropriate actions:

- As part of the proposal and contracting process, learn whether the project addresses important performance requirements and discuss alternatives for addressing those requirements. Be alert for discussions of actions you consider inappropriate.

- Examine previous organizational experiences with needs assessments and determine how the results were used. If previous needs assessments led to inappropriate actions, discuss these with the client before deciding whether or not to proceed with the proposed project.

- Examine the political situation, including the views of key stakeholders. Determine, in advance, the possibilities for inappropriate interpretations and uses of the findings.

- Keep the needs assessment focused on its stated purpose and objectives. This may be best achieved by conducting regular meetings with stakeholders to review the purpose and the current progress.

3. This book emphasizes stakeholder involvement, but how do I deal with multiple stakeholders at various levels throughout the organization?

This is a very common situation, particularly in large and complex organizations. One tip is to recognize that stakeholders can participate in various ways throughout the needs assessment process. Figure 10.1 describes an actual needs assessment that was provided by David Minger, vice president of Student Affairs at Coconino Community College. It shows one approach to encouraging many stakeholders to be involved.

Coconino Community College (CCC) is located in Coconino County in northern Arizona. At 18,617 square miles, the county is the second largest in the United States. CCC consists of two large campuses in Flagstaff, plus campuses throughout the district in Page, Williams, and Grand Canyon. Additional classes are held in Tuba City and Fredonia. The distances between campuses mean that the use of technology to deliver education, student services, and general communications is absolutely crucial. Technology is also used to build and maintain virtual teams among employees who work asynchronously and at great distances from one another.

In 2004, the Student Affairs (SA) Division set two major goals: (1) put all services online "24/7," and (2) use technology to link dispersed teams and provide team members with communications, training, and assessment tools. A needs assessment was used to achieve the goals.

Process for Technology Needs Assessment

The needs assessment involved four phases:

Staff Input

The vice president for student affairs (VPSA) conducted one-on-one interviews with all employees in the SA Division, devoting more than eighty hours over a several-month period. The interview process captured several hundred specific ideas, many of which were related to the use of technology and all of which were recorded in a database. The ideas ranged from the specific—better reports are needed in order to drop nonpaying students—to broad strategic considerations—implement plans to meet future, not just current, needs.

FIGURE 10.1 *Example of a Needs Assessment That Involved Many Stakeholders*

Informal Comparative Study of Former or Other Colleges

Learning about best practices at other colleges was addressed through staff attending conferences and by other means. The VPSA noted that the availability of technologically enhanced services at CCC varied from those at other colleges. As a result a number of services were flagged for improvement, for example, automating verification of enrollment and putting the verification service online.

Listing and Clustering the Identified Needs

The various ideas from the previously mentioned one-on-one interviews were grouped into categories. For example, all items related to admissions (for example, creating applications and new admissions reports online) were put in the same category. The result was a fifty-item document with headings and subheadings that could double as a checklist. Each of the fifty items showed a need for concrete action or resources to advance the division toward its goals.

Involving the Larger Campus Team

The next step was to bring together managers from the SA Division and experts from Information Technology Services. At their initial meeting, they worked to determine to whom each request would be referred for discussion, prioritization, and resource allocation. That conversation continues.

FIGURE 10.1 *Example of a Needs Assessment That Involved Many Stakeholders* (continued)

4. This book emphasizes stakeholder participation in the needs assessment project, but should I involve people who do not want to participate?

If the needs assessment is conducted by one person and the findings and decisions that result affect only that person, then little collaboration is required. However, we know of few such situations. More commonly, needs assessments involve multiple participants, shared decision making, and shared responsibility for ensuring that the findings of the needs assessment are implemented to produce the expected results.

Learning why the stakeholders do not want to participate is a starting point for action. Consider obtaining answers to the following questions:

- Does the individual understand the purpose and expectations for the needs assessment?

- Does the individual expect the needs assessment to result in a loss of personal power or power of a favored group?

- Is a larger social drama unfolding with increasing tension between the forces for change and the forces against change?

- Is the individual concerned that the needs assessment process may not produce accurate and appropriate findings?

- Does the individual feel that his or her opinions and insights will be ignored or used to cause personal harm or harm to others?

- Does the individual feel respected (or not respected) by the other stakeholders?

Once you know an individual's reasons for noninvolvement, you may address the issues by using the following tactics:

- Schedule a short meeting between you and the individual to clarify misunderstandings and highlight the benefits and risks of collaboration.

- Consider discussing the noninvolvement with his or her supervisor to determine whether that person can support your work.

If the above tactics seem unsuccessful and the individual's collaboration is important to the needs assessment or to implementing its findings, discuss the issue with your client and develop a solution. For example, you may consider whether to let the individual excuse him- or herself or whether other changes can be made in the needs assessment process that would encourage participation. If you decide to let individuals excuse themselves, consider how this will impact the needs assessment findings and their implementation.

5. Some authors describe needs assessment as a type of evaluation, and others describe needs assessment and evaluation as distinct processes. What is the relationship between needs assessment and evaluation?

The purpose of evaluation is to determine the merit, worth, or value of something. There are many types of evaluation (for example, formative evaluation, summative evaluation, and needs assessment). Needs assessment *is* a type of evaluation because it relies on data to determine the merit, worth, or value of various needs in a situation and to negotiate the most effective way to address those needs.

Some people also use the term *evaluation* to describe the measurement of how something was done, the efficiency and effectiveness of actions, or how well the solution produced the desired results. Thus, many HRD or HPT models show the needs assessment phase occurring at the beginning of a process and the evaluation phase occurring after an intervention has been designed, developed, and implemented. The term *evaluation* used this way can refer to measuring a needs assessment process and outcomes to determine the efficiency and effectiveness of actions and how well the process and results of the needs assessment matched the desired results.

6. What additional resources could be especially helpful when conducting a needs assessment?

Many good needs assessment resources are available. Figure 10.2 shows some of our favorites. We turn to such resources when working on a complex needs assessment or one that has high stakes for individuals or organizations. One cautionary note: authors define their terms, such as needs assessment, needs analysis, and performance analysis, in different ways.

7. This book describes formal needs assessments. Are informal needs assessments ever useful?

Yes! Informal assessments are an unspoken, natural part of communication. For example, two people meet in the hallway. One person assesses the situation, notices that the other is carrying a large stack of papers, and decides to submit an important report later.

1. **A resource with additional practical tactics and information on data-collection techniques.** *Figuring Things Out* by Zemke and Kramlinger (1982) is a golden oldie that offers practical tactics for implementing a needs assessment, such as, "Start the study as high in the organization as possible and work your way down" (p. 8). It also describes how to implement data-collection techniques, including the popular ones (for example, observation and interview) and such techniques as consensus groups, fault tree analysis, and behavioral frequency counts.

2. **A resource with additional ideas for analyzing needs and prioritizing them.** *From Needs Assessment to Action* (Altschuld & Witkin, 2000) offers many strategies for systematically analyzing needs assessment data. It also describes systematic processes for establishing priorities.

3. **Resources that describe various types of needs assessment.** Review Rossett's books, articles, and Web page. *First Things Fast* (Rossett, 1999) focuses on performance analysis, which Rossett defined as the preliminary study of a situation to determine if a more detailed training needs assessment is justified. Her Web site, http://www.josseybass.com/legacy/rossett/rossett/resources.htm, provides analysis strategies for three different types of situations: performance problems, people development, and rollouts (that is, when an organization is introducing a change).

4. **A research-based model for implementing a knowledge and skills assessment.** *The Performance Analysis for Training (PAT) Model* (Kunneman & Sleezer, 2000; Sleezer, 1990) can be a useful addition to a knowledge and skill assessment. The PAT model includes a set of worksheets that detail the phases, steps, and activities involved in determining the training needs in an organization. This is one of the few models of needs assessment that has been researched.

5. **Models of the human performance technology process.** The *Human Performance Technology Process* model (Van Tiem, Moseley, & Dessinger, 2004) at http://www.ispi.org/services/whatshptmodel.pdf shows the relationships among performance analysis; cause analysis; intervention selection, design, and development; intervention implementation and change; and evaluation.

6. **Books that describe HRD and HPT.** Two resources that discuss needs assessment as part of systematic approaches to HRD and HPT are the *Handbook of Human Performance Technology* (Pershing, 2006) and *Foundations*

FIGURE 10.2 *Additional Needs Assessment Resources*

of Human Resource Development (Swanson & Holton, 2001). If you are facing a complex situation, these resources may be especially helpful.

7. **Books that present various approaches to and tools for evaluation, including needs assessment.** Evaluation in Organizations: A Systematic Approach to Enhancing Learning, Performance, and Change (Russ-Eft & Preskill, 2001) describes various approaches to evaluation, along with a step-by-step process for designing and implementing such projects. Building Evaluation Capacity: 72 Activities for Teaching and Training (Preskill & Russ-Eft, 2005) elaborates the ideas from the previous book and provides worksheets and activities that can be used to engage stakeholders.

8. **Conferences sponsored by professional associations that have expert presentations on needs assessment.** Good places to learn about the cutting-edge thinking of practitioners include conferences that are sponsored by ASTD (www.astd.org) and the International Society for Performance Improvement (www.ispi.org). A good place to learn about new research and scholarship on needs assessment and how that affects practice is the Academy of Human Resource Development (www.ahrd.org), and a good place to learn about advances in needs assessment as part of evaluation is the American Evaluation Association (www.eval.org).

FIGURE 10.2 *Additional Needs Assessment Resources* (continued)

When assessments are shared informally with other group or organizational members, they become explicit (Jordan & Putz, 2004). The dialogue that results from sharing informal assessments can raise awareness of issues, produce information, provide support for individuals, and create the groundwork for future action.

Informal assessments are less likely to provide baseline facts and figures for evaluating future actions when they are based on flawed data collection or analysis. For example, a group of employees who discussed their unit's needs for change during their afternoon break may not realize that only those who agreed with the leader (and represented a small minority of the unit) voiced their opinions.

Another caution when using informal needs assessments is that they may lack stakeholder participation at the level required for future action.

For example, three like-minded managers decided their direct reports would comply with a new procedure. They were surprised when their employees, who were angry with the decision, made sure that the new procedure was ineffective.

Situations that are highly politicized, complex, or resource intensive usually require precise thinking, extensive negotiation, and documentation. A formal needs assessment is the right tool for such situations because it prescribes a process, documents one or more characteristics of the situation, and usually results in a report. However, in situations where there is high agreement and low costs, consider using an informal needs assessment. Also consider using informal needs assessment to get participation from stakeholders in a low-cost way.

Both formal and informal assessments are useful for investigating needs, identifying the causes of current performance, finding appropriate solutions, and building a momentum for action. Decide whether your situation requires an informal or formal needs assessment or a combination of both.

CONCLUSION

This chapter provided answers to commonly asked questions. It also identified resources that you can use to extend your needs assessment knowledge.

HRD and HPT professionals who conduct needs assessments to improve learning and performance now work in challenging times. Learning and performance improvement has become more important than ever before for individuals, groups, organizations, communities, countries, and international groups. Moreover, new strategies offer more choices than ever before for collecting and analyzing data and reporting results; new research findings present fresh insights into how to improve learning and performance; new technologies provide innovations in communication and data management.

The information presented in this chapter in combination with information from earlier chapters on needs assessment theories, approaches, data-collection and analysis strategies, and managing a needs assessment can help you plan a needs assessment and also deal with issues as they arise. In addition, Part Four contains forms to help you get started.

The assumptions and choices that you make at the beginning of learning, training, and performance improvement initiatives set their direction. This book has highlighted ways to use data to inform needs assessment assumptions and has described various choices that are available when planning and implementing a needs assessment. Given its importance to HRD and HPT initiatives, using this information to inform practice and improve the efficiency and effectiveness of needs assessments is well worth the effort.

IV

Needs Assessment Toolkit

TOOLKIT FORM 2.1 *Tools and Strategies for Assessing Systems*

Directions: Review the first column and identify the type of system pattern for your situation. Then consider the various assessment strategies and tools for that pattern.

Types of System Patterns	Assessment Strategies and Tools
Visible patterns that are easily measured	Identify the visible patterns using such complexity metaphors as the butterfly effect and edge of chaos.
	Distinguish among linear, nonlinear, and random; systemic and nonsystemic patterns.
	Use mathematical models (such as the Balanced Scorecard) to track mutually causal factors.
	Use the 15 percent concept. Gareth Morgan (2006) states that in a work situation, a person has only about 15 percent control because 85 percent of the control is shaped by the structures, systems, events, and culture in which they operate. The same is true for organizations. Morgan recommends not trying to change the 85 percent that is out of control, but instead knowing where the influence lies and where it can be exercised.
Patterns that are only partially visible or invisible, but easily measured	Become knowledgeable about the focus issue from the literature and practice, so you know where and how to look for these patterns.
	Describe or model the subtle relationships and structures that shape human system dynamics.
	Influence the self-organizing process in human systems by shifting components that are visible and that influence the nonlinear dynamics.
	Use mathematical tools to represent the subtle, nonlinear dynamics of a human system.
	Diagram a network by using network analysis as described in *Linked: The New Science of Networks* by Barabasi (2002). TouchGraph can be used to diagram networks. This open-source software package can be found at www.touchgraph.com.

TOOLKIT FORM 2.1 *Tools and Strategies for Assessing Systems* (continued)

Types of System Patterns	Assessment Strategies and Tools
	Use social network analysis tools to map and measure the informal relationships between people. These tools can reveal key value creators and informal knowledge communities that drive performance.
Patterns that are invisible and not easily measured	Use facilitated individual and group reflections to identify nonlinear dynamics.
	Use mathematical models (such as data mining, computer simulation, and artificial intelligence) to make visible the emerging patterns that are deeply embedded in the phenomena.

Note: The information in this table was adapted from Eoyang, G. (2004). Practitioner's landscape. *Emergence: Complexity & Organization, 6*(1, 2), 55–60.

TOOLKIT FORM 4.1 *Knowledge and Skills Assessment Interview Guide*

Name: _____   **Date:** _____

Interviewer: _____   **Interviewee:** _____

General Questions

1. Why do you think training is needed?

   _____

   _____

   _____

   _____

   _____

2. Describe specific instances of how workplace productivity has been affected by lack of knowledge and skills.

   _____

   _____

   _____

   _____

   _____

   _____

3. Give specific examples of how shortfalls in performance have affected unit goals, overall organization goals, or customer-satisfaction indices. (Add other indicators that are specific to your organization).

   _____

   _____

   _____

   _____

   _____

TOOLKIT FORM 4.1 *Knowledge and Skills Assessment Interview Guide*
(continued)

4. What other factors (internal or external) do you think are causing performance problems?

_____

_____

_____

_____

_____

Questions for Client Contact

5. What are the goals of the assessment?

_____

_____

_____

_____

6. What resources (monetary and nonmonetary) will be available for conducting the assessment?

_____

_____

_____

7. Whose approval must be obtained in order to proceed with the assessment?

_____

_____

_____

_____

8. Which groups must buy in to the concept?

_____

_____

_____

9. What are the most convenient times for collecting data?

_____

_____

_____

_____

10. What is the projected timeline for implementing the solutions?

_____

_____

_____

_____

11. List characteristics of the target audience, such as age, educational level, learning styles, attitudes toward learning, and computer literacy.

_____

_____

_____

_____

12. What is the approximate size of the target audience by position, geographic location, and so forth?

_____

_____

_____

_____

13. Has the target audience received prior training in this area? If so, what type of training?

_____

_____

_____

_____

14. What are the prerequisites for the program or programs?

_____

_____

_____

_____

15. Will certification be required?

_____

_____

_____

_____

16. Who are the internal and external customers of the target audience?

_____

_____

_____

_____

TOOLKIT FORM 4.2 *Skills Assessment Survey*

The Human Resources Department is conducting a survey of the job requirements of all [name of job function] at [name of company]. The information collected will be used to prepare a training plan for all [name of job function]. Your input is vital for ensuring the success of this initiative.

Instructions: This survey should take approximately fifteen to twenty minutes to complete. For each of the following items, please circle the appropriate rating. For items that are not applicable, circle "N.A." Please be candid in your responses.

Key:

1 = Very low   2 = Low   3 = Medium   4 = High   5 = Very high   N.A. = Not applicable

Current Level of Proficiency

[Enter skills here]

Example:

1. Obtain product information from customer   1   2   3   4   5   N.A.

Note: Add a place to enter demographic information.

Interpretation of Scores

All items that receive a rating of "3" or below indicate a need for training. The assumption is that the desired rating is "4" or above.

To ensure accuracy of responses, because there is a possibility that ratings may be inflated, do the following:

- Conduct follow-up interviews with unit managers to corroborate information obtained from surveys.

- Consider sending anonymous surveys. (The major disadvantage of this method is that individualized training needs cannot be identified.)

TOOLKIT FORM 4.3 *Customer-Service Knowledge and Skills Assessment Survey*

The Training Department is conducting a customer-service training needs assessment at [name of company]. The information collected will be used to prepare a training plan for all customer-service personnel. Your input is vital for ensuring the success of this initiative.

Instructions: This questionnaire will take approximately twenty-five minutes to complete. Please be candid when responding to the questions.

1. What are the five main responsibilities of your job? List the approximate percentage of time you spend on each job responsibility.

_____

_____

_____

_____

_____

2. What knowledge and skills do you require to be successful in your job?

_____

_____

_____

_____

3. What are the critical success factors for effective performance in your job?

_____

_____

_____

_____

4. What are the main barriers to your success?

_____

_____

_____

_____

TOOLKIT FORM 4.3 *Customer-Service Knowledge and Skills Assessment Survey* (continued)

5. What are the most difficult aspects of your job?

_____

_____

_____

_____

_____

6. What should the training priorities for your job function be?

_____

_____

_____

_____

_____

7. What prior customer-service training have you received? List all training received, including in previous jobs.

_____

_____

_____

_____

_____

8. What are your preferred learning styles (self-paced, computer-based, classroom)? Describe any others.

_____

_____

_____

_____

_____

Note: The following portion of the questionnaire can also be distributed to supervisors and other internal or external customers if the instructions are modified.

9. Please complete the following self-assessment, using the following scale:

1 = Very Poor   2 = Poor   3 = Average   4 = Good   5 = Excellent   N.A. = Not Applicable

a. Knowledge of customer-service standards	1	2	3	4	5	N.A.
b. Knowledge of customer-service phone etiquette	1	2	3	4	5	N.A.
c. Knowledge of products	1	2	3	4	5	N.A.
d. Knowledge of product rules and regulations	1	2	3	4	5	N.A.
e. Ability to handle customer-service calls	1	2	3	4	5	N.A.
f. Ability to respond promptly to requests	1	2	3	4	5	N.A.
g. Ability to handle customer complaints	1	2	3	4	5	N.A.
h. Ability to solve problems quickly	1	2	3	4	5	N.A.
i. Ability to make decisions quickly	1	2	3	4	5	N.A.
j. Ability to negotiate	1	2	3	4	5	N.A.
k. Ability to listen carefully	1	2	3	4	5	N.A.
l. Ability to manage stress	1	2	3	4	5	N.A.

[Add questions of your own.]

Name: _____   Date: _____

Position/Title: _____   Unit: _____

TOOLKIT FORM 4.4 *Management Knowledge and Skills Assessment Survey*

The Training Department is conducting a company-wide training needs assessment at [name of company]. The information collected will be used to prepare a training plan for all [name of job function] personnel. Your input is vital for ensuring the success of this initiative.

Instructions: This questionnaire will take approximately twenty-five minutes to complete. Please be candid when responding to the questions.

1. What are the five main responsibilities of your job? List the approximate percentage of time you spend on each job responsibility.

_____

_____

_____

_____

_____

2. What knowledge and skills do you require to be successful in your job?

_____

_____

_____

_____

3. What are the critical success factors for your effective performance?

_____

_____

_____

_____

4. What are the main barriers to your success?

_____

_____

_____

_____

TOOLKIT FORM 4.4 *Management Knowledge and Skills Assessment Survey*
(continued)

5. What are the most difficult aspects of your job?

_____

_____

_____

_____

_____

6. What should the training priorities for your job function be?

_____

_____

_____

_____

_____

7. What prior management training have you received? List all such training received, including in previous jobs.

_____

_____

_____

8. What are your preferred learning styles (self-paced, computer-based, classroom)? Describe any others.

_____

_____

_____

_____

_____

Name: _____ Date: _____

Position/Title: _____ Unit: _____

Instructions: This survey will take only a short time to complete. Please rate your [managers/subordinates] on the following items, using the key below. Please be candid when responding. Circle your choices.

Key: 1 = Strongly Disagree   2 = Disagree   3 = Somewhat Agree
4 = Agree   5 = Strongly Agree   N.A. = Not Applicable

Leadership

1. They are visionaries.	1	2	3	4	5	N.A.
2. They serve as coaches and mentors.	1	2	3	4	5	N.A.
3. They encourage teamwork.	1	2	3	4	5	N.A.
4. They treat me and my coworkers fairly.	1	2	3	4	5	N.A.
5. They treat me and my coworkers with respect.	1	2	3	4	5	N.A.
6. They project a positive view of the organization to clients and customers.	1	2	3	4	5	N.A.

Communication

7. They clearly communicate what is expected of me.	1	2	3	4	5	N.A.
8. They clearly communicate what is expected of my coworkers.	1	2	3	4	5	N.A.
9. They keep me informed about critical business issues that may have an impact on my job.	1	2	3	4	5	N.A.
10. They keep me updated about the unit's accomplishments through memos and other communication channels.	1	2	3	4	5	N.A.
11. They are effective in making presentations to others.	1	2	3	4	5	N.A.
12. They establish clear channels of communication between group members.	1	2	3	4	5	N.A.
13. They establish clear channels of communication between this unit and other units.	1	2	3	4	5	N.A.

Performance Management

14. They are genuinely concerned about my job performance.	1	2	3	4	5	N.A.

TOOLKIT FORM 4.4 *Management Knowledge and Skills Assessment Survey*
(continued)

Key: 1 = Strongly Disagree 2 = Disagree 3 = Somewhat Agree
4 = Agree 5 = Strongly Agree N.A. = Not Applicable

15. They provide me and my coworkers with challenging tasks.	1	2	3	4	5	N.A.
16. They provide opportunities for professional growth and development.	1	2	3	4	5	N.A.
17. They conduct effective performance appraisal meetings.	1	2	3	4	5	N.A.
18. They resolve conflicts effectively.	1	2	3	4	5	N.A.
19. They provide feedback at the appropriate time.	1	2	3	4	5	N.A.

Project Management

20. They delegate tasks according to the appropriate skill and experience level of the group members.	1	2	3	4	5	N.A.
21. They effectively forecast the workload of the group.	1	2	3	4	5	N.A.
22. They plan effectively.	1	2	3	4	5	N.A.
23. They take appropriate corrective action when necessary.	1	2	3	4	5	N.A.

Customer Service

24. They put the customers' needs before the needs of the organization.	1	2	3	4	5	N.A.
25. They are sensitive to the needs of customers.	1	2	3	4	5	N.A.
26. They are continually seeking ways to provide superior service to customers.	1	2	3	4	5	N.A.
27. They are aware of industry standards for customer service.	1	2	3	4	5	N.A.

Sales

28. They demonstrate effective negotiation skills.	1	2	3	4	5	N.A.
29. They proactively identify sales opportunities with internal and external customers.	1	2	3	4	5	N.A.
30. They forge strong relationships with internal and external customers.	1	2	3	4	5	N.A.

TOOLKIT FORM 4.5 *Knowledge and Skills Assessment Curriculum Plan*

	Core Curriculum		
	Year 1	**Year 2**	**Year 3**
Sales Executive			
Sales Manager			
Sales Associate			

TOOLKIT FORM 4.5 *Knowledge and Skills Assessment Curriculum Plan* (continued)

	Advanced Curriculum		
	Year 1	Year 2	Year 3
Sales Executive			
Sales Manager			
Sales Associate			

TOOLKIT FORM 5.1 *Job Analysis Questionnaire*

Purpose: The purpose of this questionnaire is to gather information about your job.

Directions: Answer all the questions. Return the survey to [name/ department] by [date].

Name: _____

Sample Questions:

1. List all your major responsibilities. Then prioritize each item by assigning a number to it. For example, assign "1" to the responsibility you consider most important.

_____

_____

_____

_____

_____

_____

_____

_____

2. Why are these responsibilities important to your job?

_____

_____

_____

_____

_____

_____

TOOLKIT FORM 5.1 *Job Analysis Questionnaire* (continued)

3. What equipment and tools do you use in your job?

_____

_____

_____

_____

_____

_____

_____

4. Describe some specific duties or tasks you perform in your job that are related
to your major responsibilities. List the responsibilities you mentioned previously.
After you indicate the specific duty or task, please state how often you perform this
duty or task.

_____

_____

_____

_____

_____

_____

_____

5. What knowledge do you require to perform your job successfully?

_____

_____

_____

_____

_____

_____

TOOLKIT FORM 5.1 *Job Analysis Questionnaire* (continued)

6. What qualities are necessary to make you successful in your job?

_____

_____

_____

_____

_____

_____

7. What prior knowledge, skills and abilities, or attitudes did you bring to your position that helped to make you successful in your job?

_____

_____

_____

_____

_____

_____

8. List any courses, workshops, or training programs you attended in the past that you feel have helped you succeed in your job.

_____

_____

_____

_____

_____

_____

_____

_____

TOOLKIT FORM 5.1 *Job Analysis Questionnaire* (continued)

9. Describe any other contributing factors you feel have made you successful in your job.

_____

_____

_____

_____

_____

_____

_____

_____

_____

_____

TOOLKIT FORM 5.2 *Job Training and Non-Training Recommendations I
(Professional/Supervisory/Management)*

Job Title (Professional/Supervisory/Management):
Department:
Location:

Job Responsibility 1 _____

  1. Job Task: _____
  2. Job Task: _____
  3. Job Task: _____
  4. Job Task: _____
  5. Job Task: _____
Competencies: _____
Training Requirements: _____
Non-Training Requirements: _____

Job Responsibility 2 _____

  1. Job Task: _____
  2. Job Task: _____
  3. Job Task: _____
  4. Job Task: _____
  5. Job Task: _____
Competencies: _____
Training Requirements: _____
Non-Training Requirements: _____

Job Responsibility 3 _____

  1. Job Task: _____
  2. Job Task: _____
  3. Job Task: _____
  4. Job Task: _____
  5. Job Task: _____
Competencies: _____
Training Requirements: _____
Non-Training Requirements: _____

TOOLKIT FORM 5.2 *Job Training and Non-Training Recommendations I (Professional/Supervisory/Management)* (continued)

Job Title (Professional/Supervisory/Management):
Department:
Location:

Job Responsibility 4 _____

  1. Job Task: _____

  2. Job Task: _____

  3. Job Task: _____

  4. Job Task: _____

  5. Job Task: _____

Competencies: _____

Training Requirements: _____

Non-Training Requirements: _____

Job Responsibility 5 _____

  1. Job Task: _____

  2. Job Task: _____

  3. Job Task: _____

  4. Job Task: _____

  5. Job Task: _____

Competencies: _____

Training Requirements: _____

Non-Training Requirements: _____

Job Responsibility 6 _____

  1. Job Task: _____

  2. Job Task: _____

  3. Job Task: _____

  4. Job Task: _____

  5. Job Task: _____

Competencies: _____

Training Requirements: _____

Non-Training Requirements: _____

TOOLKIT FORM 5.3 *Job Training and Non-Training Recommendations II (Administrative)*

Job Title (Administrative):
Department:
Location:

Job Responsibility 1 _____

1. Job Task: _____

2. Job Task: _____

3. Job Task: _____

4. Job Task: _____

Knowledge: _____

Skills/Abilities: _____

Attitudes: _____

Behaviors: _____

Standards: _____

Training Requirements: _____

Non-Training Requirements: _____

Job Responsibility 2 _____

1. Job Task: _____

2. Job Task: _____

3. Job Task: _____

4. Job Task: _____

Knowledge: _____

Skills/Abilities: _____

Attitudes: _____

Behaviors: _____

Standards: _____

Training Requirements: _____

Non-Training Requirements: _____

TOOLKIT FORM 5.3 *Job Training and Non-Training Recommendations II (Administrative)* (continued)

Job Title (Administrative):
Department:
Location:

Job Responsibility 3 _____

1. Job Task: _____

2. Job Task: _____

3. Job Task: _____

4. Job Task: _____

Knowledge: _____

Skills/Abilities: _____

Attitudes: _____

Behaviors: _____

Standards: _____

Training Requirements: _____

Non-Training Requirements: _____

Job Responsibility 4: _____

1. Job Task: _____

2. Job Task: _____

3. Job Task: _____

4. Job Task: _____

Knowledge: _____

Skills/Abilities: _____

Attitudes: _____

Behaviors: _____

Standards: _____

Training Requirements: _____

Non-Training Requirements: _____

TOOLKIT FORM 5.4 *Job Task Analysis Checklist*

_____ Assemble project team.

_____ Select above-average high performers and/or subject-matter experts who will provide input for the work session.

_____ Notify employees' supervisors.

_____ Conduct briefing if necessary.

_____ Prepare job analysis questionnaire.

_____ Distribute or mail questionnaires.

_____ Summarize questionnaires.

_____ Prepare flip chart for session. List key job responsibilities supplied by all participants.

_____ Prepare agenda for work sessions.

_____ Obtain materials for session.

_____ Prepare meeting room for session.

_____ During session, refine list of job responsibilities.

_____ Create task statements for each job responsibility.

_____ Omit nonessential tasks.

_____ Identify knowledge, skills, and abilities required to perform tasks.

_____ Identify training requirements to perform job tasks.

_____ Prioritize training needs.

_____ Prepare draft of job training plan.

_____ Submit draft of job training plan to supervisors for approval.

_____ Prepare final draft of job training plan.

_____ Distribute copies of final job training plan.

TOOLKIT FORM 6.1 *Competency Project Plan Worksheet—Detailed Schedule of Events*

Task	SC	PL	HRM	SM 1	SM 2	C	TP	Completion Date
Subtotal: (Hours)								

Project Members: (Enter names of project members here)

Key: SC = Steering Committee   PL = Project Liaison   HRM = Human Resource Manager
      SM 1 = Sales Manager 1   SM 2 = Sales Manager 2   C = Client
      TP = Training Professional

TOOLKIT FORM 6.2 *Competency Interview Worksheet*

Name of Interviewer: _____   Date: _____

I. About the Interviewee

Name: _____   Position: _____

Unit: _____   Highest Degree: _____

Previous Training Received: _____

_____

_____

II. About the Interviewee's Job

Name of Manager: _____   Number of Subordinates: _____

Previous Jobs (Year, Position, Company, Location):

_____

_____

_____

_____

_____

_____

_____

_____

1. What are the five main responsibilities of your job?

_____

_____

_____

_____

_____

_____

_____

_____

TOOLKIT FORM 6.2 *Competency Interview Worksheet* (continued)

2. What skills and abilities do you require to accomplish each of the above?

_____

_____

_____

_____

_____

_____

3. What other skills and abilities do you require to make yourself successful in your job?

_____

_____

_____

_____

_____

_____

III. About the Interviewee's Work Experiences

4. Think about an incident you experienced that resulted in a successful outcome. What was the context? When did it happen? Who was involved?

_____

_____

_____

_____

_____

_____

_____

5. What did you feel or think?

_____

_____

_____

_____

_____

_____

_____

_____

_____

_____

6. What did you say? Why were these actions and words effective?

_____

_____

_____

_____

_____

_____

_____

_____

_____

7. What were the results? What significance does this event have?

_____

_____

_____

_____

_____

_____

_____

8. Think about an incident you experienced that resulted in an unsuccessful outcome. What was the context? When did it happen? Who was involved?

_____

_____

_____

_____

_____

_____

_____

_____

_____

_____

_____

_____

_____

_____

_____

_____

_____

_____

9. What did you feel or think?

_____

_____

_____

_____

_____

_____

_____

10. What did you say? Why were these actions and words ineffective?

_____

_____

_____

_____

_____

_____

_____

11. What are some other actions you did not take at the time that could have helped you succeed?

_____

_____

_____

_____

_____

_____

_____

12. What were the results? What significance does this event have?

_____

_____

_____

_____

_____

_____

_____

TOOLKIT FORM 6.3 *Competency Dictionary Worksheet*

1.

Core Clusters	Definitions

2.

Core Clusters	Definitions

3.

Core Clusters	Definitions

TOOLKIT FORM 6.3 *Competency Dictionary Worksheet* (continued)

4.

Core Clusters	Definitions

5.

Core Clusters	Definitions

6.

Core Clusters	Definitions

TOOLKIT FORM 6.4 *Competency Model Worksheet*

Dimensions	Competencies/Core Clusters			
	Position 1	Position 2	Position 3	Position 4
1.				
2.				
3.				
4.				
5.				
6.				

TOOLKIT FORM 6.5 *Individual Learning Development Plan for* _____ (Year)

Employee Name: _____

Business Unit: _____

Position: _____

Manager: _____

Competency to Be Developed	Learning and Development Activities	Internal and External Support and Resources Needed	Success Measures	Completion Date	Review Date

Employee Signature: _____   Date: _____

Manager Signature: _____   Date: _____

TOOLKIT FORM 7.1 *Business Issues Worksheet*

To examine an existing performance problem

1. What are the key business issues that must be addressed?

_____

_____

_____

2. How long have the problems existed?

_____

_____

_____

3. What are the consequences of not solving these problems?

_____

_____

_____

4. Which business processes are affected by the problems?

_____

_____

_____

5. What are the performance improvement goals?

_____

_____

_____

6. What is preventing these goals from being achieved?

_____

_____

_____

TOOLKIT FORM 7.1 *Business Issues Worksheet* (continued)

To address a future performance need

1. What are the key business issues that must be addressed?

_____

_____

_____

_____

2. Why must these issues be addressed?

_____

_____

_____

_____

3. Which business processes are currently affected?

_____

_____

_____

_____

4. What are the performance improvement goals?

_____

_____

_____

_____

5. What is preventing these goals from being achieved?

_____

_____

_____

_____

This form describes eight models that can be used to map organizational performance. A brief description introduces each and space for taking additional notes follows each. Use these models, individually or in combination, to consider the various relationships among aspects of performance, how performance improvements at one level actually combine to create performance improvements at another level, and whether the necessary performance supports are in place.

Models 1 through 4 focus on relationships among aspects of performance at the same hierarchical level within an organization (that is, the individual level, the group level, or the organizational level). Models 5, 6, and 7 focus on how phenomena at one level can affect the performance of interest at another level. Model 8 integrates Models 1 through 4 and Model 5.

Model 1: Organization Level Performance

This model shows processes that occur among the aspects of performance at the highest level in an organization. Each solid arrow in Figure 1 indicates the direction of the process among the aspects of performance. For example, the arrow between capacity and production process reflects the process that occurs when organizational resources are used to create products or services.

The dotted circle represents the organization's permeable boundary. The thick shaded arrows show exchanges with the external resource and product markets. The resource market is the competitive space where the organization obtains land, capital, natural resources, and so forth. The product market is the competitive space where the organization interacts with customers and receives economic rents for its products and services. Economic rents are the returns received in excess of the cost of creating the product or service.

The organization's capacity includes the resources that were obtained from the resource market or from organizational members and that can be selected to produce a product or service. The organization's accomplishments garner economic rents that flow back into organization capacity, and experience that contributes to the learning process. Organizational performance also depends on the performance that occurs at the individual and the group levels. Performance at these levels is shown in Models 2, 3, and 4.

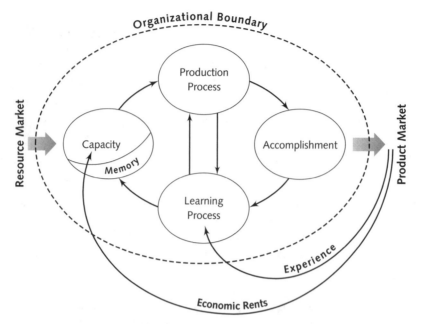

FIGURE 1 *Aspects of Organization Level Performance*

Notes on aspects of organizational level performance:

_____

_____

Model 2: Individual Level Performance

Each individual is a distinct unit who combines his or her personal resources (individual capacity) with the resources provided by the organization (such as tools, data, and raw materials) to produce value-enhanced accomplishments that are deployed to other parts of the organization. Individual accomplishments become the resources that fuel the production process of other individuals and groups, thus creating a value-added chain. The individual production process adds value to a portion of the final organizational accomplishment that is instrumental to the organization's performance. The overlap of individual and organizational capacity in Figure 2 depicts that when an individual learns by engaging in the production process or by evaluating accomplishments, the initial learning is stored in the individual's memory and contributes to organizational memory if shared. Knowledge held by an individual can be viewed as part of the organization's aggregate capacity (but not necessarily organizational memory, because most of this knowledge is lost to the organization if the individual leaves).

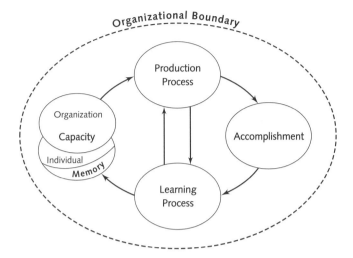

FIGURE 2 *Aspects of Individual Level Performance*

Notes on aspects of individual level performance:

_____

_____

Models 3 and 4: Group Level Performance

This level is very complex, as shown in Model 3 (see Figure 3). Each dot represents an individual who operates in the manner described at the individual level. Moreover, the individuals could be operating at different speeds and be at different stages in the performance cycle.

The clusters of dots enclosed with dashed lines represent groups. The overlapping clusters show individuals who have multiple relationships.

Performance at the group level also includes the aspects of performance (see Model 4 in Figure 4). Capacity at the group level includes group member skills, abilities, and knowledge as well as resources provided by the organization. It also includes resources that result from interactions among individuals within the group and that enable the group to produce accomplishments that the same individuals working alone could not attain.

The group production process involves individuals working together in value-enhanced ways that are unavailable to the group's individual members. The group's accomplishments become resources to other parts of the organization, where they lead to further enhancement in a value-adding chain. The group receives feedback from the production processes and from

TOOLKIT FORM 7.2 *Fisher's Models of Organizational Performance Worksheet* (continued)

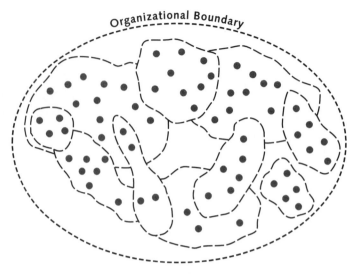

FIGURE 3 *Complexity at the Group Level*

Notes on aspects of complexity:

_____

_____

_____

comparisons with set standards; this feedback results in new knowledge that may be used to improve group production processes and thus enhance the value of group accomplishments. The new knowledge that a group acquires by evaluating its accomplishment and by reflecting on the feedback from the production process may become organizational memory via sharing and formal documentation.

Model 5: Compositional Links Among Performance Levels

Use a compositional link when performance at one level combines to create performance at a higher level. For example, a firm's organizational climate for innovation reflects the shared perceptions of all the employees in a firm. Compositional links occur within the same aspect of performance. As an example, the model in Figure 5 shows the compositional links for the capacity aspect of performance. One arrow shows the link that could occur if individual contributions combine to create organization capacity; another arrow shows the link that could occur if individual contributions combine to create group capacity; and a third arrow shows the link that could occur if group contributions combine to create organization capacity. For more information on compositional links see Klein and Kozlowski (2000).

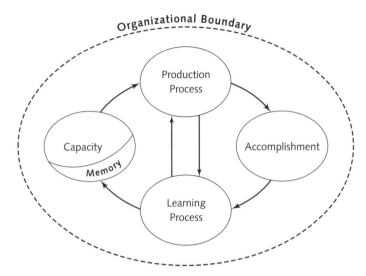

FIGURE 4 *Aspects of Group Level Performance*

Notes on aspects of group level performance:

_____

_____

_____

FIGURE 5 *Compositional Links Among Performance Levels*

Notes on compositional links that are relevant to the need:

_____

_____

_____

Model 6: Cross-Level, Multi-Aspect Links

Some relationships link both the levels and the aspects of performance. The model in Figure 6 shows a sample of these relationships for two aspects of performance: capacity and process. Individual capacity may affect group production when individual skills contribute to the group process. Individual capacity may directly affect organizational production process (such as an expert technician's role). Organization capacity contributes to individual production when the individual uses the organization's pool of resources (such as computers) to do work. Group capacity influences the individual's production process when an individual, as part of a group process, learns skills that he or she then transfers to the individual production process.

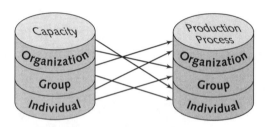

FIGURE 6 *Example of Cross-Level, Multi-Aspect Links*

Notes on cross-level, multi-aspect links:

_____

_____

_____

Model 7: Hybrid Relationships

This model (see Figure 7) introduces the notion of hybrid relationships. In such cases, performance at one level affects performance at another level, which in turn affects a process. For example, an individual can share an idea that modifies a group's production process. As another example, a group can brainstorm ideas that modify the organization's production process. Closer inspection shows that hybrid links are actually combinations of the compositional and intralevel links described earlier. In each example, the sharing of resources with others is at the core of the relationship.

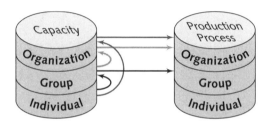

FIGURE 7 *Example of Hybrid Links*

Notes on hybrid links:

_____

_____

_____

Model 8: Intralevel and Compositional Relationships

To aid in understanding, Model 8 shows the intralevel and compositional relationships described in Models 1, 2, 4, and 5 (see Figure 8). Note that to keep the figure legible, the relationships between top management and the product and resource markets are not shown. The arrows between the aspects of performance depict process transfers at all three levels.

*Note that earlier versions of this information were published in Fisher and Sleezer (2003).

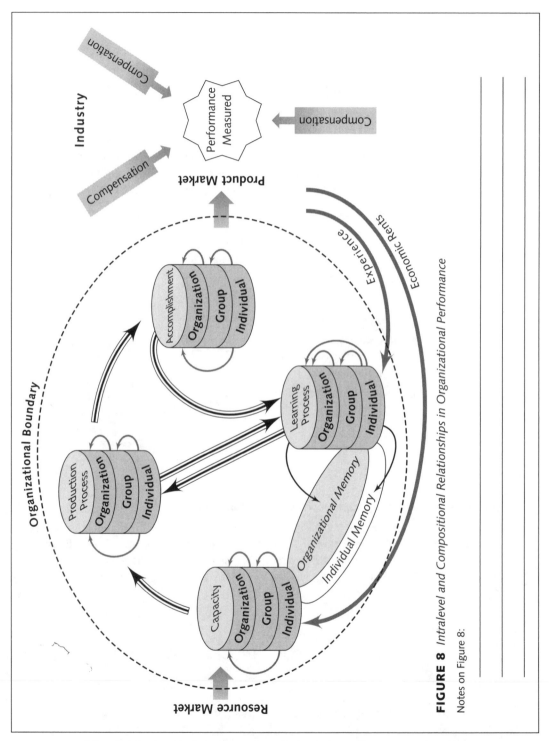

FIGURE 8 *Intralevel and Compositional Relationships in Organizational Performance*

Notes on Figure 8:

_____

_____

_____

_____

TOOLKIT FORM 7.3 *Process Map Worksheet*

A process map shows the steps or activities that are being performed in a business process. A process boundary shows where a business process begins and ends. For example, the process boundary for order management begins when a customer-service unit sends a mail order and ends when a product is received by a customer.

Instructions

1. To show information received from a source OUTSIDE a process boundary, such as a customer, customer request, or another business unit, use a RECTANGLE.

2. To show any activity that is being carried out WITHIN a process, such as completing a form, use an OVAL.

3. To show the FLOW between activities (INPUTS and OUTPUTS), use an ARROW.

Tips for Process Mapping

1. Document steps in sequence. Try to restrict your diagram to major steps at first. Do not become bogged down in too much detail.

2. Begin by identifying the first major process activity, such as processing quotes, as shown in the attached figure. Determine the flow of information to and from this process. Use single-pointed arrows for information that flows in one direction. For information that flows in both directions between two units or processes, use two-pointed arrows.

3. Identify the next major process. Document the inputs and outputs to this process.

4. Link all major processes as well as inputs and outputs. If you cannot define intermediate steps, make notes. Come back to this step later.

5. When you have finished creating your process map, retrace steps to verify accuracy of information collected.

TOOLKIT FORM 7.3 *Process Map Worksheet*
(continued)

Process: _____

Questions To Ask

1. What is the sequence of activities that must be performed to complete this process?
2. Who performs each activity?
3. How much time does it take to perform each activity or step?
4. What are the external inputs?
5. Where do internal inputs come from?
6. What are the outputs?
7. Where do the outputs go?

Key:

⬜ Department or Unit
⬭ Processing Activity
→ Flow of Information in One Direction
↔ Flow of Information in Both Directions

TOOLKIT FORM 7.4 *Gap Analysis Worksheet*

Process	Current Performance Indicators	Gap	Effect

TOOLKIT FORM 7.5 *Change Readiness Checklist*	
	Have clear objectives for the change initiative been established?
	Has a leader been assigned to facilitate the change effort?
	Does the leader have the requisite interpersonal and organization development skills to facilitate the change initiative?
	Are adequate internal resources available for implementing the performance improvement plan?
	Are external resources required?
	Have reasons for change been communicated to top management?
	Is top management committed to implementing the performance improvement plan?
	Is top management willing to take risks to implement the performance improvement plan?
	Have reasons for change been communicated to middle management?
	Is middle management committed to implementing the performance improvement plan?
	Have reasons for change been communicated to frontline employees?
	Are frontline employees committed to implementing the performance improvement plan?
	Have milestones for celebrating successes been established?
	Have strategies for motivating and reinforcing those involved in the performance improvement initiative been devised?
	Has a follow-up plan to monitor the change initiative been developed?

TOOLKIT FORM 7.6 *Performance Improvement Planner*

Project Identification Number: _____

Project Description: _____

Project Sponsor (Name/Business Unit): _____

Performance Improvement Goal: _____

_____

_____

Critical Success Factors: _____

_____

_____

_____

Obstacles to Success: _____

_____

_____

_____

Prerequisites for Starting the Project: _____

_____

_____

Project Structure: _____

_____

_____

Team Requirements: _____

_____

Resources: _____

_____

Expected Cost: _____

_____

Benefits: _____

_____

_____

_____

TOOLKIT FORM 7.6 *Performance Improvement Planner* (continued)

Timeline

Milestone	Expected Start Date	Expected Completion Date
1. _____		
2. _____		
3. _____		
4. _____		
5. _____		
6. _____		

Completed By: _____   Approved By: _____

Date: _____   Date: _____

TOOLKIT FORM 8.1 *Needs Assessment Checklist*

The following checklist may be used for a variety of needs assessments, including the four approaches presented in this book. Because the assessment requirements for each situation differ, use the items that are most applicable to your organization's needs. Also, note that some needs assessments have additional steps that are not included in this checklist.

Gather Preliminary Data

	1. Have you had preliminary meetings to gather information from your client contact and other key people?
	2. Have you considered the ethical issues that may arise while gathering preliminary data and the ethical codes that can guide your actions?
	3. Have you obtained senior management's perspectives about the goals of the assessment?
	4. Have you identified the attitudes of learners and other stakeholders toward the needs assessment and the new program, system, training, or technology?
	5. Is there consensus about the goals of the needs assessment among those involved?
	6. Do you have a holistic perspective about the project, the organization, and its larger environment?
	• How does this project fit with other organizational efforts?
	• How do the organization's systems, culture, and politics support the project?
	• Have you identified what factors are likely to impede the needs assessment or the project?
	• Have you identified the prerequisites for installing, developing, using, revising, or updating the program, system, training, or technology?
	• Have you identified whether changes are needed that are complementary to the effort you are working on (for example, changes in work design, rewards, tools, culture, training, or environment)?

	• If complementary changes are needed, do you know who is responsible for implementing and monitoring the changes?
	• Have you identified the educational level of the target audience?
	• Have you determined learners' preferred learning styles?
	• Have you identified the computer literacy levels of the target audience?
	7. Have you determined what testing or evaluation strategies will be used to measure success?
	8. Have you determined whether certification will be required?
	9. Have you identified resources that are available to conduct and implement the assessment?
	10. Do you require the assistance of external sources, such as subject-matter experts or consultants?
	11. Have you reviewed records, reports, and other pertinent extant data?
	12. Have you obtained input from all other pertinent sources, such as units, archives, and internal or external sources?
	13. Have you determined what kind of needs assessment you will conduct (that is, job and task, knowledge and skill, competency, or strategic analysis)?

Plan the Assessment

	14. Have you established a project plan?
	15. Have you established a system for managing the needs assessment?
	16. Have you determined what types of data must be collected?
	17. Have you identified multiple sources of data?
	18. Have you identified multiple data-gathering methods that will be effective?

	TOOLKIT FORM 8.1 *Needs Assessment Checklist* (continued)
	19. Have you designed the process or processes for collecting and storing data?
	20. Have you established a mechanism for tabulating and analyzing results?
	21. Have you developed a plan for having the appropriate people review the draft data analysis?
	22. Have you considered the ethical guidelines that should be followed when planning and implementing this plan?
	23. Have you notified the appropriate people about the assessment?
	24. Have you obtained approval to proceed with the assessment?
Data Collection	
	25. Have you developed the needs assessment tools?
	26. Have you validated the needs assessment tools?
	27. Have you pilot-tested the needs assessment tools?
	28. Do you have a system for managing the collected data?
	29. Have you scheduled the data collection?
	30. Have you communicated the purpose and process of the data collection with those who will participate in it?
Analyze Data	
	31. Have you compiled results?
	32. Have you identified patterns and deviations in data?
	33. Have you organized the data for review by the client and stakeholders?
	34. Have you briefed your client contact and senior management about the draft results of the assessment?

TOOLKIT FORM 8.1 *Needs Assessment Checklist* (continued)

Prepare Final Report and Presentation

	35. Have you established priorities for implementing the solutions identified by the needs assessment?
	36. Have you estimated projected costs and benefits for implementing each solution?
	37. Does the report contain all the relevant information?
	38. Is the report accurate, precise, and concise?
	39. Is the report format appropriate for the audience and organization?
	40. Have you included all the appropriate supporting documents in the appendix?

TOOLKIT FORM 8.2 *Needs Assessment Proposal Template*

Replace the information in the brackets with information specific to your project.

Proposal: [Title of the needs assessment]

Submitted to: [Client's name]
[Client's title]
[Client's address]
[Client's phone/e-mail number]

Submitted by: [Analyst's name]
[Analyst's title]
[Analyst's address]
[Analyst's phone number/e-mail address]

Date: [Date proposal is submitted to client]
[Name of Proposal] Page 2

TOOLKIT FORM 8.2 *Needs Assessment Proposal Template* (continued)

Purpose

[Insert one to two paragraphs with background information about the organization and the reason for conducting the needs assessment.]

[Insert one paragraph that overviews the needs assessment, describes how it will accomplish the purpose, and refers to the table on the next page.]

Staffing

The analyst for this project, [insert consultant's name], has [insert brief description of the analyst's experience/education/certification in needs assessment].

Cost

The costs for the needs assessment are [insert per hour costs or total project costs]. In addition, the organization will pay for such agreed-upon expenses as [specify expenses the organization will pay]. The organization will also provide the analyst with [specify the services that the organization will provide for the needs assessment, such as transportation, copying, mailing, and printing]. [Specify the work that the analyst will do at the organization] will be done on-site; however, [specify the needs assessment work that will not be completed at the worksite] will be completed off-site. This contract can be renegotiated at any time as needed.

TOOLKIT FORM 8.2 *Needs Assessment Proposal Template* (continued)

Projected Needs Assessment Phases, Outcomes, and Timelines

	Phase 1: [title]	Phase 2: [title]	Phase 3: [title]	Phase 4: [title]	Phase 5: [title]
Purpose	[Insert the purpose of the phase.]	[Insert the purpose of the phase.]	[Insert the purpose of the phase.]	[Insert the purpose of the phase.]	[Insert the purpose of the phase.]
Process	[Insert the steps required to complete the phase.]	[Insert the steps required to complete the phase.]	[Insert the steps required to complete the phase.]	[Insert the steps required to complete the phase.]	[Insert the steps required to complete the phase.]
Outcome	[Insert the expected outcome or outcomes.]	[Insert the expected outcome or outcomes.]	[Insert the expected outcome or outcomes.]	[Insert the expected outcome or outcomes.]	[Insert the expected outcome or outcomes.]
Projected Due Date	[Insert the expected completion date for the phase.]	[Insert the expected completion date for the phase.]	[Insert the expected completion date for the phase.]	[Insert the expected completion date for the phase.]	[Insert the expected completion date for the phase.]

TOOLKIT FORM 8.3 *Needs Assessment Report Template*

Directions: Replace the information in the brackets with information specific to your project.

Report Title: [for example, Phase I Report, Final Report, etc.]

Submitted to: [Client's name]
[Client's title]
[Client's address]
[Client's phone number/e-mail address]

Submitted by: [Analyst's name]
[Analyst's title]
[Analyst's address]
[Analyst's phone number/e-mail address]

Date: [Date proposal is submitted to client]

Executive Summary

[Insert one or two sentences that overview what was accomplished in this reporting period.] [Insert one sentence stating why this accomplishment is important for the project and organization.] The following sections summarize the goals, process, findings, and recommendations for this phase.

Goals

1. [List a goal for the project or phase here.]
2. [List another goal for the project or phase here.]
3. [Continue listing project goals.]

Process

1. [List a process step for the project or phase here.]
2. [List another process step for the project or phase here.]
3. [Continue listing process steps and writing descriptions as needed.

Findings

1. [List a finding for the project or phase here.]
2. [List another finding for the project or phase here.]
3. [Continue listing findings as needed.]

Recommendations

[Summarize the recommendations for the phase and project, which are based on the findings, in one or two paragraphs.]

TOOLKIT FORM 8.3 *Needs Assessment Report Template* (continued)

[Title of the phase or project]

Goal

The goals of this phase were:

1. [List a goal here.]
2. [List another goal here.]

(See Attachment A: Projected Needs Assessment Phases, Processes, Outcomes, and Timelines.)

Process

Completing this phase of the needs assessment involved [summarize the process steps that were used to complete this phase. These should match the steps that are listed in Attachment A.]

Findings

[Summarize all findings here.]

Recommendations

[Report all recommendations here.]

Attachment A: Projected Needs Assessment Phases, Processes, Outcomes, and Timelines

TOOLKIT FORM 8.3 *Needs Assessment Report Template* (continued)

Projected Needs Assessment Phases, Outcomes, and Timelines

	Phase 1: [title]	**Phase 2: [title]**	**Phase 3: [title]**	**Phase 4: [title]**	**Phase 5: [title]**
Purpose	[Insert the purpose of the phase.]	[Insert the purpose of the phase.]	[Insert the purpose of the phase.]	[Insert the purpose of the phase.]	[Insert the purpose of the phase.]
Process	[Insert the steps required to complete the phase.]	[Insert the steps required to complete the phase.]	[Insert the steps required to complete the phase.]	[Insert the steps required to complete the phase.]	[Insert the steps required to complete the phase.]
Outcome	[Insert the expected outcome or outcomes.]	[Insert the expected outcome or outcomes.]	[Insert the expected outcome or outcomes.]	[Insert the expected outcome or outcomes.]	[Insert the expected outcome or outcomes.]
Projected Due Date	[Insert the expected completion date for the phase.]	[Insert the expected completion date for the phase.]	[Insert the expected completion date for the phase.]	[Insert the expected completion date for the phase.]	[Insert the expected completion date for the phase.]

Glossary

Accomplishments	The outputs resulting from certain actions and behaviors.
Actuals	Current performance or knowledge (Rossett, 1987).
Anonymity	Characteristic of information such that its source (the author or the person who generated it) is not known.
Anticipated needs	Needs that are expected to prevail in the future.
Behavior	Actions of a person, or what people do (Harless, 1970).
Behavioral interviews	A data-collection method that obtains information about what high performers do that makes them successful and what low performers do that makes them fail. (*See also* Critical incident.)
Brainstorming	A method of problem solving in which group members contribute ideas spontaneously, and these ideas are not initially judged.
Business goal	A statement describing a measure or target for an organization or a business unit that will be achieved during a certain period.
Business process	A series of activities that provide products, deliver services, or manage resources.

Business strategies	The sets of policies, plans, and directions that the organization uses to achieve its business goals.
Business unit	A department or function within an organization.
Closed-ended question	A question containing specific options from which a respondent must choose, such as a multiple-choice question.
Comparative needs	Needs occurring among two or more entities with similar characteristics.
Competency	A knowledge, skill, or attitude that enables a person to perform effectively the activities of a given occupation or to function to the standards expected in employment (International Board of Standards for Training, Performance, and Instruction, 2005).
Competency dictionary	An organized list of definitions for individual competencies.
Competency model	A composite picture or conceptual framework of the competencies necessary for people to be successful in a job function.
Confidentiality	The specifics of what is seen or heard is kept private and not shared with anyone.
Conflict of interest	A clash between one's personal interests and one's professional position.
Consultant	Someone who has influence in a situation but does not have the power to make changes or implement programs directly (Block, 2000).
Core cluster	Competencies grouped together under a broad dimension.
Cost-benefit analysis	A comparison of the costs and benefits for one or more options.

Critical incident	Process of collecting information about important (critical) performance in special situations (incidents) (Flanagan, 1954, 1974).
Critical-incident needs	Needs that become apparent after system failures.
Curriculum	An overall plan containing the objectives, course modules, content outline, and delivery strategies for training or educational programs.
Deficiency	How a situation deviates (in a negative direction) from the ideal (Harless, 1970).
Domain	A cluster of related competencies grouped together under a broad dimension.
Downsizing	A reduction in the number of personnel within an organization; also called a *reduction in force* or RIF.
Environment	Conditions surrounding performance, such as the work environment, equipment, tools, or machinery used in performing tasks (Harless, 1970).
Ethics	A set of principles or values, in this case the principles guiding the conduct of professionals undertaking needs assessments.
Expressed needs	Needs that are evident (e.g., demands for a product or service exceed supply).
Evaluation	A process for determining and reporting on the merit, worth, or value of needs or of a program, process, or product.
Formative evaluation	An evaluation whose purpose is to identify possible modifications for improving a program, process, or product.
Needs assessment	A process for figuring out the gap between the current condition and the desired condition (called a need) and how to address the need and close the gap.

Summative evaluation	An evaluation whose purpose is to make a final judgment on the merit, worth, or value of a program, process, or product.
Extant data	A term given to quantitative and qualitative information used during the course of a needs assessment; these data already exist in documents and records.
Felt needs	Needs that reflect what people think they need.
Fill-in-the-blank question	An open-ended question that limits the length of responses.
Focus group	A data-collection method in which the opinions of five to eight people who share similar expertise (such as operations staff) are sought.
Gap	Difference between what is and what should be, between an actual state (what results are) and a desired state (what results should be) (Kaufman, Rojas, and Mayer, 1993).
High performers	People who consistently exceed expectations and are informally labeled "masters" or experts by their peers and managers.
Human system dynamics	The field that explores the underlying forces that shape the ever-emerging and dynamic patterns of human systems of all sizes.
Individual learning development plan	A plan that is developed for a person and shows the learning activities, support and resources, success indicators, and measures for improving performance.
Interval scales	A series of marks that is used to record information. The information can come from a closed-ended question. This numeric information possesses the following characteristics: (1) the points on the scale

	appear in an increasing (or decreasing) order and (2) there exists an equal distance between points on the scale.
Interventions	Activities that interfere so as to modify a process or situation. For example, organization development consultants use such interventions as teambuilding and culture change to modify the process or situation in the client's context.
Interviews	A data-collection method used with individuals that can be conducted in person, by phone, or by computer technology (such as online cameras and videoconferencing).
Semi-structured interviews	A list of objectives with corresponding questions initially guides the interview; the interviewer spontaneously asks supplemental questions to further explore areas of interest.
Structured interviews	A list of objectives, a corresponding list of questions, and in some cases, a corresponding list of responses to questions that guide the interview process.
Unstructured interviews	Questions are not listed in advance of the interview; rather, a list of objectives and the topics to be covered guide the interview.
Job analysis	A process of gathering, organizing, evaluating, and reporting work-related information.
Job function expert	Someone within or outside the organization who is considered an expert or highly skilled in a particular job task.
Job responsibility	The scope of activities for a job function or job position, such as operations manager.

Job task	What must be done in order to fulfill a responsibility—usually there are four to six tasks for each responsibility.
Job task statement	The what, why, and how of a job.
Knowledge	The body of facts about a subject matter and the understanding that a person acquires through study or experience. What people must know, such as subject matter, concepts, or facts, in order to do a job.
Learning	The gaining of knowledge, understanding, skills, and abilities; is not observable.
Learning channel	A way of acquiring knowledge, understanding, skills, and abilities.
Likert-type scale	A scale on which respondents are asked to rate values or attitudes (Likert, 1932).
Mission	A broad statement describing an organization's future plans and directions.
Multiple-choice question	A type of closed-ended question that includes a list of three or more options from which respondents select one or more responses.
Need	A learning or performance gap that exists between the current condition and the desired condition.
Needs assessment	A diagnostic process that relies on data collection, collaboration, and negotiation to identify and understand gaps in learning and performance and to determine future actions.
Needs assessment proposal	A document that specifies the project's purpose, phases, processes, expected outcomes, timeline, and expenses. When approved, the proposal serves as a contract.

Network	A complex, interconnected group or system.
Nominal scale	A series of marks that is used to record information. Each mark has a name (e.g., bad, average, good, and so forth), but the choices are not arranged in any prescribed order.
Normative needs	Needs that arise when an individual or group is not meeting one or more established standards.
Observation	A type of data collection that involves the watching, inspecting, and taking note of behaviors and the environment.
Open-ended question	A question that a respondent answers in his or her own words.
Optimals	Desired knowledge or performance (Rossett, 1987).
Performance	Behaviors and their resulting accomplishments and capacities; performance, unlike learning, is observable.
Performance improvement planner	A blueprint that documents all the performance improvement projects that must be undertaken to improve the overall effectiveness of an organization.
Performance statement	An explanation or elaboration of the activities that constitute a competency statement and provide specifics of the larger competency.
Pilot test	A trial run in which an object, such as a data-collection instrument, is tested for problems or "bugs."
Position training plan	A matrix of the knowledge, skills, and abilities needed for an individual to perform a job.
Process boundary	An arbitrary "line" that shows where a business process begins and ends.

Process map

A graphical illustration of the steps or activities that are performed in a business.

Project creep

Expansion of or increase in a project that occurs when the scope of a project keeps growing.

Project shrink

Contraction of or reduction in a project that occurs when the scope of the project keeps getting smaller.

Qualitative data

Data that are not numeric; can be words, diagrams, or pictures.

Quantitative data

Data that can be expressed in numeric form, such as indices, sales averages, or number of word-processing programs used.

Reliability

The level of consistency in the item or the data; reflects the level of error in the measurement.

Return on investment (ROI)

Net program benefits divided by program costs multiplied by 100.

Root cause analysis

A systematic procedure for identifying the most probable cause of problems so organizational leaders can eliminate them rather than continue to deal with their symptoms. The process involves continuing to ask "Why?" until the pattern becomes evident and the causes of the problem become obvious.

Self-organization

The tendency for complex adaptive systems to generate new organizational forms spontaneously when pushed far from equilibrium.

Skills or abilities

Knowledge that one proficiently applies in appropriate situations; what people must do in order to perform a job.

Social network theory	Analysis technique that depicts social relationships using nodes and ties. Nodes are the individual entities within a network; ties are the relationships between the entities. A social network maps all the relevant ties between the nodes that are being studied. A social network analysis can provide both a visual and a mathematical analysis of human relationships.
Stakeholders	People who have a stake in the outcomes of a needs assessment; the findings and recommendations may affect them or their work.
Standard	A criterion that specifies how a task should be performed.
Survey	A data-collection method typically used to gather data from many people at one time; can be mailed, e-mailed, or offered online.
Task analysis	A method of determining the knowledge, skills, tools, conditions, and requirements needed to perform a job.
Training	A process that supports individual learning (a gain in knowledge and skills) through specialized instruction and practice.
Trustworthiness	The level of confidence that we can trust particular data (typically qualitative) to provide insight into "truth" or "reality." The procedures used to collect and analyze data affect trustworthiness of the data. For example, data that are collected and analyzed using sloppy procedures are not trustworthy.
Two-choice question	A closed-ended question the answer to which can be either one thing or the other (e.g., yes/no, true/false), and the responses are mutually exclusive.

Validity	The level of confidence we can have that specific data provide insight into "truth" or "reality." Procedures that are used to collect and statistically analyze data (typically quantitative) affect the validity of the resulting data.
Want	Something the client would like to have even though it does not contribute to the learning or performance goal.
Worthy performance	The ratio of valuable accomplishments to costly behaviors (Gilbert, 1978).

References

CHAPTER ONE

Mathews, B. P., Ueno, A., Kekale, T., Repka, M., Pereira, Z., & Silva, G. (2001). Quality training: Needs and evaluation-findings from a European survey. *Total Quality Management, 12*(4), 483–490.

Preskill, H., & Russ-Eft, D. (2003). A framework for reframing HRD evaluation practice and research (pp. 199–257). In A. M. Gilley, L. Bierema, & J. Callahan (Eds.), *Critical issues in HRD.* Cambridge, MA: Perseus.

Russ-Eft, D., & Preskill, H. (2005). In search of the holy grail: ROI evaluation in HRD. *Advances in Developing Human Resources, 7*(1), 71–85.

Scriven, M. (1991). *Evaluation thesaurus* (4th ed.). Thousand Oaks, CA: Sage.

CHAPTER TWO

Eoyang, G. (2004). Practitioner's landscape. *Emergence: Complexity & Organization, 6*(1, 2), 55–60.

Gilbert, T. J. (1978). *Human competence: Engineering worthy performance.* New York: McGraw Hill.

Hale, J. A. (2005). The future of ISD—Death if we keep killing it. Paper presented at International Society for Performance Improvement conference, Dallas.

Harless, J. (1970). *An ounce of analysis (is worth a pound of objectives).* Newman, GA: Harless Performance Guild.

Kaufman, R. (1992). *Strategic planning plus: An organizational guide.* Newbury Park, CA: Sage.

Kaufman, R. (2005). Defining and delivering measurable value: A mega thinking and planning primer. *Performance Improvement Quarterly, 18*(3), 6–16.

Mager, R. F., & Pipe, P. (1984). *Analyzing performance problems; Or, you really oughta wanna* (2nd ed.). Belmont, CA: Pitman Management and Training.

Phillips, J. J., & Phillips, P. P. (2005). *Measuring return on investment (ROI) basics.* Alexandria, VA: American Society for Training and Development.

Rummler, G. A., & Brache, A. P. (1995). *Improving performance: How to manage the white space in the organization chart.* San Francisco: Jossey-Bass.

Swanson, R. A., & Gradous, D. B. (1990). *Forecasting the financial benefits of human resource development.* San Francisco: Jossey-Bass.

CHAPTER THREE

Callahan, M. (1985, February). Be a better needs analyst. *Infoline 8502.* Alexandria, VA: American Society for Training and Development.

Dillman, D. A. (2000). *Mail and internet surveys: The tailored design method* (2nd ed.). Hoboken, NJ: Wiley.

Gayeski, D. (2004, November). Goin' mobile. *T + D, 58*(11), 46–51.

Guba, E. G., & Lincoln, Y. S. (1981). *Effective evaluation: Improving the usefulness of evaluation results through responsive and naturalistic approaches.* San Francisco: Jossey-Bass.

Krueger, R. A., & Casey, M. A. (2000). *Focus groups* (3rd ed.). Thousand Oaks, CA: Sage.

Likert, R. (1932). A technique for the measurement of attitudes. *Archives of Psychology, 140,* 1–55.

Paul, K., & Bracken, D. (1995, January). Everything you always wanted to know about employee surveys. *Training and Development, 49*(1), 47.

Phillips, J. J., & Holton, E. F., III. (Eds.) (1995). *In action: Conducting needs assessment.* Alexandria, VA: American Society for Training and Development.

Robinson, D., & Robinson, J. (1989). *Training for impact.* San Francisco: Jossey-Bass.

Rossett, A. (1987). *Training needs assessment.* Englewood Cliffs, NJ: Educational Technology Publications.

Russ-Eft, D., & Preskill, H. (2001). *Evaluation in organizations: A systematic approach to enhancing learning, performance, and change.* Cambridge, MA: Perseus.

Schwarz, R. (1995, May). Hiring good facilitators. *Training and Development, 49*(5), 67.

CHAPTER FOUR

Holton, E. F., III (Ed.) (1995). *In action: Conducting needs assessment.* Alexandria, VA: American Society for Training and Development.

McLean, G. N. (2005). *Organization development: Principles, processes, performance.* San Francisco: Berrett-Koehler.

Robinson, D. G., & Robinson, J. C. (1995). *Performance consulting: Moving beyond training.* San Francisco: Berrett-Koehler.

Russ-Eft, D., & Preskill, H. (2001). *Evaluation in organizations: A systematic approach to enhancing learning, performance, and change.* Cambridge, MA: Perseus.

CHAPTER FIVE

Brannick, M. T., & Levine, E. L. (2002). *Job analysis: Methods, research, and applications for human resource management in the new millennium.* Thousand Oaks, CA: Sage.

Butruille, S. (1989, March). Be a better job analyst. *Infoline 8903.* Alexandria, VA: American Society for Training and Development.

Callahan, M. (1985, March). Be a better task analyst. *Infoline 8503.* Alexandria, VA: American Society for Training and Development.

Fine, S. A., & Cronshaw, S. F. (1999). *Functional job analysis: A foundation for human resources management.* Mahwah, NJ: Lawrence Erlbaum.

Shepherd, A. (2001). *Hierarchical task analysis.* New York: Taylor & Francis.

Swanson, R. A. (1994). *Analysis for improving performance. Tools for diagnosing organizations and documenting workplace expertise.* San Francisco: Berrett-Koehler.

CHAPTER SIX

Bergmann, H., Hurson, K., & Russ-Eft, D. (1999). *Everyone a leader: A grassroots model for the new workplace.* Hoboken, NJ: Wiley.

Boyatzis, R. (1982). *The competent manager.* Hoboken, NJ: Wiley.

Flanagan, J. C. (1954). The critical incident technique. *Psychological Bulletin, 51,* 327–358.

Flanagan, J. C. (1974). *Measuring human performance.* Palo Alto, CA: American Institutes for Research.

Griffiths, B. (1997, February). *Constructing and validating a competency model.* Unpublished manuscript.

International Board of Standards for Training, Performance, and Instruction® (2005). *Glossary of terms.* Retrieved September 6, 2005, from http://www.ibstpi.org.

Klein, J. D., Spector, J. M., Grabowski, B. L,, & de la Teja, I. (2004). *Instructor competencies: Standards for face-to-face, online, and blended settings* (3rd ed.). Greenwich, CT: Information Age.

Marrelli, A. F. (1998). An introduction to competency analysis and modeling. *Performance Improvement, 37*(5), 8–17.

McClelland, D. C. (1973). Testing for competence rather than for "intelligence." *American Psychologist, 28,* 1–14.

McLagan, P. (1980, December). Competency models. *Training and Development, 34*(12), 23.

Richey, R. C., Fields, D. C., & Foxon, M. (2001). *Instructional design competencies: The standards.* Syracuse, NY: ERIC Clearinghouse on Information & Technology, Syracuse University.

Rothwell, W. J. (1996). *ASTD models for human performance improvement: Roles, competencies, and outputs.* Alexandria, VA: American Society for Training and Development.

Russ-Eft, D. (2004). Customer service competencies: A global look. *Human Resource Development International, 7,* 211–231.

Spencer, L. M., & Spencer, S. M. (1993). *Competence at work: Models for superior performance.* Hoboken, NJ: Wiley.

White, R. W. (1959). Motivation reconsidered: The concept of competence. *Psychological Review, 66,* 297–333.

CHAPTER SEVEN

Fisher, S. R. (2000). *A multilevel theory of organizational performance.* Doctoral dissertation, Oklahoma State University, Stillwater.

Fisher, S. R., & Sleezer, C. M. (2003). *An overview of a multilevel theory of organizational performance.* Paper presented at Institute of Behavioral and Applied Management conference, Tampa, FL.

Gephart, M. A., & Van Buren, M. E. (1996, October). Building synergy: The power of high-performance work systems. *Training & Development, 50*(10), 21–36.

Mankins, M. C., & Steele, R. (2005, July–August). Turning great strategy into great performance. *Harvard Business Review, 83*(7/8), 64–72.

Porter, M. E. (1980). *Competitive strategy.* New York: Free Press.

Robinson, D., & Robinson, J. (2006). The art and the science of performance consulting. *Performance Improvement, 45*(4), 5–8.

Rummler, G. A., & Brache, A. P. (1995). *Improving performance: How to manage the white space in the organization chart.* San Francisco: Jossey-Bass.

Swanson, R. A. (1996). *Analysis for improving performance: Tools for diagnosing organizations and documenting workplace expertise.* San Francisco: Berrett-Koehler.

CHAPTER EIGHT

Block, P. (2000). *Flawless consulting* (2nd ed.). San Francisco: Jossey-Bass.

International Board of Standards for Training, Performance, and Instruction®. (2005). Evaluator competencies. Retrieved 9/1/06 from www.ibstpi.org.

King, S. B. (1998). *Practitioner verification of the human performance improvement analyst competencies and outputs.* Doctoral dissertation, Pennsylvania State University. *Digital Dissertations,* AAT 9915873.

McNamara, C. (2005). *Field guide to consulting and organizational development with nonprofits.* Minneapolis: Authenticity Consulting, LLC.

Phillips, J. J. (2003). *Return on investment in training and performance improvement programs* (2nd ed.). Burlington: MA: Butterworth-Heinemann.

Rothwell, W. J. (1996). *ASTD models for human performance improvement: Roles, competencies, and outputs.* Alexandria, VA: American Society for Training and Development.

Swanson, R. A., & Gradous, D. B. (1990). *Forecasting the financial benefits of human resource development.* San Francisco: Jossey-Bass.

Torres, R. T., Preskill, H., & Piontek, M. (2005). *Evaluation strategies for communicating and reporting: Enhancing learning in organizations* (2nd ed.). Thousand Oaks, CA: Sage.

CHAPTER NINE

American Evaluation Association (2004). *Guiding principles for evaluators.* Retrieved July 25, 2006, from http://www.eval.org/Publications/GuidingPrinciples.asp.

International Society for Performance Improvement (2002). *Code of ethics.* Retrieved July 25, 2006, from www.ispi.org.

Joint Committee on Standards for Educational Evaluation (1994). *The program evaluation standards: How to assess evaluations of educational programs.* Thousand Oaks, CA: Sage.

Russ-Eft, D., Burns, J. Z., Dean, P. J., Hatcher, T. G., Otte, F. L., & Preskill, H. S. (1999). Academy of Human Resource Development Standards on Ethics and Integrity. Bowling Green, OH: AHRD. Retrieved 7/25/06 from www.ahrd.org.

CHAPTER TEN

Altschuld, J. W., & Witkin, B. R. (2000). *From needs assessment to action: Transforming needs into solution strategies.* Thousand Oaks, CA: Sage.

Jordan, B., & Putz, P. (2004). Assessment as practice: Notes on measures, tests, and targets. *Human Organization, 63*(3), 346–358.

Kunneman, D. E., & Sleezer, C. M. (2000). Using performance analysis for training in an organization implementing ISO-9000 manufacturing practices: A case study. *Performance Improvement Quarterly, 13*(4), 47–66.

Pershing, J. A. (2006). *Handbook of human performance technology* (3rd ed.). San Francisco: Wiley.

Preskill, H., & Russ-Eft, D. (2005). *Building evaluation capacity: 72 activities for teaching and training.* Thousand Oaks, CA: Sage.

Rossett, A. (1999). *First things fast.* San Francisco: Jossey-Bass.

Russ-Eft, D., & Preskills, H. (2001). *Evaluation in organizations: A systematic approach to enhancing learning, performance, and change.* Cambridge, MA: Perseus.

Sleezer, C. M. (1990). *The development and validation of a performance analysis for training model* (vols. 1–3). Doctoral dissertation, University of Minnesota. *Digital Dissertations,* AAT 9100979.

Swanson, R. A., & Holton, E. F., III. (2001). *Foundations of human resource development.* San Francisco: Berrett-Koehler.

Van Tiem, D. M., Moseley, J. M., & Dessinger, J. C. (2004). *Fundamentals of performance technology* (2nd ed.). Silver Spring, MD: International Society for Performance Improvement.

Zemke, R., & Kramlinger, T. (1982). *Figuring things out: A trainer's guide to needs and task analysis* (4th ed.). Reading, MA: Addison-Wesley.

TOOLKIT FORMS

Barabasi, A. (2002). *Linked: The new science of networks.* Cambridge, MA: Perseus.

Fisher, S. R., & Sleezer, C. M. (2003). *An overview of a multilevel theory of organizational performance.* Paper presented at Institute of Behavioral and Applied Management Conference, Tampa, FL.

Klein, K. J., & Kozlowski, S. W. J. (2000). *Multilevel theory, research, and methods in organizations: Foundations, extensions, and new directions.* San Francisco: Jossey-Bass.

Morgan, G. (2006). *Provocative ideas: The 15% concept.* Retrieved 7/6/06 from http://www.imaginiz.com/.

GLOSSARY

Block, P. (2000). *Flawless consulting* (2nd ed.). San Francisco: Jossey-Bass.

Flanagan, J. C. (1954). The critical incident technique. *Psychological Bulletin, 51,* 327–358.

Flanagan, J. C. (1974). *Measuring human performance.* Palo Alto, CA: American Institutes for Research.

Gilbert, T. J. (1978). *Human competence: Engineering worthy performance.* New York: McGraw-Hill.

Harless, J. (1970). *An ounce of analysis (is worth a pound of objectives).* Newman, GA: Harless Performance Guild.

International Board of Standards for Training, Performance, and Instruction (2005). *Glossary of terms.* Retrieved September 6, 2005 from http://www.ibstpi.org.

Kaufman, R., Rojas, A. M., & Mayer, H. (1993). *Needs assessment: A user's guide.* Englewood Cliffs, NJ: Educational Technology Publications.

Likert, R. (1932). A technique for the measurement of attitudes. *Archives of Psychology, 140,* 1–55.

Rossett, A. (1987). *Training needs assessment.* Englewood Cliffs, NJ: Educational Technology Publications.

Index

D

About the Authors

KAVITA GUPTA has developed training programs for corporations and conducted workshops for several universities in New England. She has been an active member of the American Society for Training and Development and has served on several boards. Ms. Gupta has also published several articles. She holds a master's degree in instructional systems technology from Indiana University.

CATHERINE (CATHY) M. SLEEZER is the human resource manager for learning and organization development at Centrilift, a division of Baker Hughes. She has consulted with many organizations in the private, public, and government sectors to address their learning and performance needs. Ms. Sleezer has also taught needs assessment courses at the master's and doctoral levels and conducted needs assessment research. She is a certified performance technologist. She is a former board member of the Academy of Human Resource Development and a former member of the ASTD Research Committee. Her previous books include *Human Resources Development Review: Research and Implications* (Sage), *Human Resource Development and Information Technology: Making Global Connections* (Kluwer), and *Improving Human Resource Development through Measurement* (ASTD).

DARLENE F. RUSS-EFT is associate professor of adult education and higher education leadership in the College of Education at Oregon State University, where she teaches master's and doctoral courses in research, program evaluation, and learning theory. Her most recent books are *Building Evaluation Capacity: 72 Activities for Teaching and Training* (Sage) and *Evaluation in Organizations: A Systematic Approach to Enhancing Learning, Performance, and Change* (Perseus Press). She is currently vice president for research for the Academy of Human Resource Development and a director and board member of the International Board of Standards for Training, Performance, and Instruction, where she is leading a team to determine evaluator competencies. From 2002 to 2005 she was editor of *Human Resource Development Quarterly.* Prior to joining the faculty of Oregon State University, in 2002, she was director of research at AchieveGlobal, Inc., and division director of research for Zenger-Miller, Inc.

How to Use the CD-ROM

SYSTEM REQUIREMENTS

PC with Microsoft Windows 98SE or later
Mac with Apple OS version 8.6 or later

USING THE CD WITH WINDOWS

To view the items located on the CD, follow these steps:

1. Insert the CD into your computer's CD-ROM drive.

2. A window appears with the following options:

   Contents: Allows you to view the files included on the CD-ROM.
   Software: Allows you to install useful software from the CD-ROM.
   Links: Displays a hyperlinked page of websites.
   Author: Displays a page with information about the author(s).
   Contact Us: Displays a page with information on contacting the publisher or author.
   Help: Displays a page with information on using the CD.
   Exit: Closes the interface window.

If you do not have autorun enabled, or if the autorun window does not appear, follow these steps to access the CD:

1. Click Start -› Run.

2. In the dialog box that appears, type d:‹<\\><\\>›start.exe, where d is the letter of your CD-ROM drive. This brings up the autorun window described in the preceding set of steps.

3. Choose the desired option from the menu. (See Step 2 in the preceding list for a description of these options.)

IN CASE OF TROUBLE

If you experience difficulty using the CD-ROM, please follow these steps:

1. Make sure your hardware and systems configurations conform to the systems requirements noted under "System Requirements" above.

2. Review the installation procedure for your type of hardware and operating system. It is possible to reinstall the software if necessary.

To speak with someone in Product Technical Support, call 800-762-2974 or 317-572-3994 Monday through Friday from 8:30 a.m. to 5:00 p.m. EST. You can also contact Product Technical Support and get support information through our website at www.wiley.com/techsupport.

Before calling or writing, please have the following information available:

- Type of computer and operating system.
- Any error messages displayed.
- Complete description of the problem.

It is best if you are sitting at your computer when making the call.